I Love
KOREA!

Edited by

Andrew C. Nahm, Ph.D.
B. J. Jones, Ph.D.
Gi-eun Lee

HOLLYM

The Romanization System and Pronunciation Guide

The Romanization system of writing Korean words used in this book is the Ministry of Education's Romanization system, which is a modified system of the McCune-Reischauer Romanization system.

Generally, the basic vowels, *a, e, i, o,* and *u* are pronounced as in Italian and Spanish:

a as in father   *e* as in end
i as in India   *o* as in Ohio
u as in rule

Two vowels, *ŏ* and *ŭ* are pronounced as below:

ŏ as *u* in but   *ŭ* as *oo* in foot

Some diphthongs (compound vowels) are pronounced as a single vowel:

ae as the *a* in apple *oe* as ö in German

But, each vowel in certain other diphthongs are pronounced separately:

ai as the *ie* in tie   *oi* as the *oy* in toy

Generally, unaspirated consonants are pronounced softly:

ch as j   *k* as g   *p* as b   *t* as d

When these consonants are aspirated by adding an apostrophe (') behind the letter, they are pronounced as in English words:

ch' as ch   *k'* as k   *p'* as p   *t'* as t

An apostrophe is also used to separate two consonants sounds as in the cases of *Tan'gun* and *han'gŭl,* etc.

Certain compound consonants are pronounced as follows:

ss as the *s* in Sam   *tch* as the *j* in jam
tt as the *d* in dam

Illustrations by

Lee Gi-eun (Pages 14-16, 28-29, 31-33, 74-75)
Pak Yo-han (Page 63)
Kim Yŏn-gyŏng (Pages 38-43, 50-55)
Chŏng Shi-rang (Pages 65-68, 80-83)
Lee Chŏng-hwa (Pages 6-7, 17-19, 45-46, 56, 64, 72-73, 76-77)
Lee Chong-du (Pages 36-37)
Ryu Chae-su (Pages 26-27)
Kang Mi-sun (Pages 20-25)
Han Yu-min (Pages 8-13, 48, 86)

Cover Illustration by
Ryu Chae-su

Copyright © 1991
by Hollym Corporation; Publishers

First published in 1991
Ninth printing, 1997
by Hollym International Corp.
18 Donald Place, Elizabeth, NJ 07208 U.S.A.
Phone: (908)353-1655   Fax:(908)353-0255

Published simultaneously in Korea
by Hollym Corporation; Publishers
13-13 Kwanchol-dong, Chongno-gu, Seoul 110-111, Korea
Phone: (02)735-7554   Fax: (02)730-5149

ISBN: 0-930878-87-6
Library of Congress Catalog Card Number: 91-76851

Printed in Korea

Contents

Arirang is one of the most popular folk songs which has a certain historical sentimentality for the Korean people.

Arirang

아 리 랑

Korean Folk Song

A - ri-ra-ang A - ri-ra-ang A - ra-a-a-ri-i Yo —
아 - 리 랑 - 아 - 리 랑 - 아 라 리 요 -

A - ri-ra-ang Ko-o-gae-e-ro-o Nŏ - mŏ-gan Ta —
아 - 리 랑 - 고 개 로 - 넘 - 어간 다 -

Na - rŭl Pŏ - ri - go Ka-shi-nŭn-ni-im ŭn —
나 - 를 버 리 고 가 시 는 님 - 은 -

Shim - ni-do-o Mo-ot-ka-a-sŏ-ŏ Pal - pyŏl-nan Ta —
십 - 리 도 - 못 - 가 서 - 발 - 병난 다 -

Arirang

A-ri-rang, A-ri-rang, A-ra-ri-yo, A-ri-rang Pass is the long road you go.
If you leave and forsake me, my own, Ere three miles you go,
lame you'll have grown.

Korea, the Nation of Good Manners

IN ancient Chinese historical records, Korea was called the Eastern Kingdom. According to Korean mythology, Tan'gun, a descendant of the gods, was the first king who ruled over this country that we now know as Korea. This country was called the nation of good manners because its people were respectful, well-mannered, and polite. It was recorded that the country was strong, but not arrogant or boastful of its strength. Its military power was great, but it never used its power to invade other countries.

동방에 오래된 나라가 있었다.
단군이라는 신선이 처음 있어 동쪽 나라의 왕이 되었다.
나라의 힘이 비록 크나 교만하거나 자랑하지 아니하였고, 군사의 힘이 강하였으나 남의 나라를
침략하지 않았고, 풍속이 아름다워 길을 갈 때는 먼저 가시라고 양보하고, 가히 예절 바른 나라니라.

Hwanung is descending from heaven to enlighten the inhabitants on earth. This is a legend which tells the story of the founding of the first Korean kingdom long ago. It also tells that all Koreans share the same bloodline of Tan'gun. Such a legend has played an important role in uniting the Korean people whenever their country faced difficulties.

The Story of Tan'gun

Long, long ago, Hwanin, who ruled heaven had a son named Hwanung. Hwanung always looked down on earth from heaven. There were many beautiful mountains, rivers, and plains on earth. Among those mountains was one named T'aebaek.

Knowing that Hwanung wished to go down and rule the people, Hwanin decided to send his son to earth and said:

"My son, I know that you have great plans for human beings on earth. Receive these heavenly seals and go."

"Thank you, Father," said Hwanung. "I will go there and enlighten the inhabitants on earth and teach them how to live."

After this, Hwanung took three sacred seals and three thousand followers and left heaven for earth. He landed on the top of Mount T'aebaek where a sacred tree had stood. It was the place where the people on earth had worshiped heaven. Arriving there, he called the place the Divine City, and made it his base to rule over human beings. He commanded the gods of wind, rain, and clouds, taught human beings how to grow food, healed the sick, and gave them 360 rules for orderly life.

When he was doing all these things, a bear and a tiger, who lived in a cave near the Divine City and wished to be human beings, came to Hwanung every day and begged him to make them human.

In the end, Hwanung gave each of them a stalk of mugwort plant and twenty pieces of garlic, and told them that if they ate them and avoided the sunlight for one hundred days, they would become human.

아득한 옛날입니다. 하늘나라를 다스리는 환인에게 환웅이라는 아들이 있었습니다.

환웅은 하늘나라에서 늘 땅의 나라를 내려다보았습니다.

그 곳에는 아름답게 펼쳐진 산과 강과 들과 그 가운데 태백이라는 산이 있었습니다.

환인은 아들 환웅이 땅의 세계에 내려가 인간을 다스려보고자 하는 마음을 헤아렸습니다.

그러던 어느 날 환인은 환웅을 불러 이야기하였습니다.

"환웅아, 네가 인간세상을 그리워하며 그들을 위해 가지고 있는 뜻을 내 알고 있느니라.

자, 이 천부인을 받아라."

"아버님, 감사합니다. 미개한 인간들을 깨우치고 사람답게 사는 방법을 가르치겠사옵니다."

환웅은 신령스러운 천부인 세 개와 무리 3천을 거느리고, 천공을 헤치며, 태백산 꼭대기 신단수 (하느님께 제사 지내는 단에 서 있는 나무)에 내려왔습니다. 그리고 그 곳을 '신시'라 부르며 세상을 다스릴 근거지로 삼았습니다.

환웅은 바람의 신, 비의 신, 구름의 신을 거느리고, 생명과 농사, 질병, 형벌, 선과 악 등 인간의 360여 가지 일들을 맡아서 세상을 다스렸습니다.

그 때 신시 근처에 곰 한 마리와 호랑이 한 마리가 한 동굴 속에서 살고 있었습니다. 곰과 호랑이는 사람이 되고 싶었습니다. 그래서 날마다 환웅을 찾아가 사람이 되게 해 달라고 빌었습니다.

환웅은 곰과 호랑이에게 신령스러운 쑥 한 줌과 마늘 20쪽을 주면서 이것을 먹고 100일 동안 햇빛을 보지 않으면 사람이 된다고 일렀습니다.

The bear and the tiger ate only the mugwort plant and garlic and stayed in the cave. It was not easy for them to do so. In fact, the tiger could not withstand the hardship and he went out after a few days. But the bear patiently remained in the cave.

곰과 호랑이는 동굴 속에서 나오지 않고 쑥과 마늘만 먹고 지냈습니다.
캄캄한 동굴 속에서 쓰디쓴 쑥과 마늘만 먹고 지내기란 몹시 힘든 일이었습니다.
며칠이 지난 어느 날, 호랑이는 견디다 못해 그만 동굴 밖으로 뛰쳐나가고 말았습니다.
그렇지만 곰은 호랑이가 나간 뒤에도 동굴 속에서 참고 기다렸습니다.

11

A surprising thing happened.
On the one hundredth day
the bear turned into a beautiful woman.
She built a small hut on a quiet and
beautiful spot and lived there, but as the days
passed she became lonely. Her loneliness increased
to the point she could no longer endure it, so she
went to see Hwanung again and begged earnestly:
"Lord Hwanung, thank you for making me a
human. Would you please find me a husband to keep
me company?" Hearing this, Hwanung pitied her,
and changed his own form into a strong and
handsome young man. After that, he made
the young woman his wife and they had
a son named Tan'gun who became
the ancestor of the Koreans.

드디어 놀라운 일이 일어났습니다.
곰은 100일 만에 아름다운 여자의 몸으로 변하였습니다.
곰에서 여인으로 변한 웅녀는, 조용하고 경치가 아름다운 곳에서
움막집을 짓고 살았습니다. 그러나 웅녀는 날이 갈수록 점점 외로워지고
적적해서 견딜 수가 없었습니다.
웅녀는 다시 환웅을 찾아갔습니다.
"환웅님, 저를 사람으로 만들어 주신 환웅님, 저에게 함께
살아갈 지아비를 점지해 주십시오." 웅녀는 간절히 빌었습니다.
환웅은 웅녀가 가엽게 느껴져서 잠시 모습을 바꾸어 건장하고 늠름한
청년이 되었습니다. 그리고 웅녀와 결혼을 하여 이내 아들을 낳았습니다.
이 아기가 바로 한국인의 시조인 단군입니다.

Tan'gun grew up strong, and in 2333 B.C., over 4,300 years ago, he established a new nation. This was the first kingdom that emerged in the Korean Peninsula, and its name was Chosŏn. After that, Tan'gun ruled over the country for 1,500 years, and then became a mountain god at the age of 1,908.

단군은 무럭무럭 자라 기원 전 2333년 즉, 지금으로부터 약 4300년 전에 나라를 세웠습니다.

이것이 한국 땅에 세워진 최초의 나라이며, 그 이름을 '조선'이라 하였습니다. 단군은 천오백 년 동안 나라를 다스렸습니다. 그 뒤 세상일에서 벗어나 산신이 되었는데, 그 때 단군의 나이가 천구백 팔 세였다고 합니다.

이 이야기는 한국인이 모두 한 핏줄임을 생각하게 하고, 하늘이 선택하여 일찍부터 나라를 세운 훌륭한 민족임을 말해 줍니다. 또한 한국이 어려움을 당할 때 국민을 모두 하나로 뭉치게 하는 가장 중요한 힘이 되고 있습니다.

This poem is taken from Songs of the Dragons Flying in Heaven, *which was compiled during the reign of King Sejong (r. 1418-50).*

A Korean Proverb

A tree with deep roots
Stands firm in the storm;
It bears abundant flowers and fruit.

뿌리가 깊은 나무는

바람에 움직이지 않으므로

꽃 좋고 열매 많으니라.

A spring with a deep source of water
Does not dry up in time of drought;
Its water becomes a river, and
Flows into the sea.

샘이 깊은 물은

가뭄에 끊이지 않으므로

내가 되어 바다에 가느니라.

14

Han'gŭl, the Korean Alphabet

EACH people has its own written language.
Han'gŭl is Korea's very own, unique writing system.
There is no other writing system like it. *Han'gŭl* means
the unique, the greatest and the best letters.

사람들은 민족이나 나라에 따라 서로 다른 글자를 쓰고 있습니다.
한글은 한국말을 적는 한국 고유의 글자입니다.
　한글은 이 세상에 단 하나밖에 없는 으뜸가는 글자이며, 큰 글자이며, 바른
글자라는 뜻입니다. 한글은 세계 어떤 문자도 쉽게 표기할 수 있습니다.

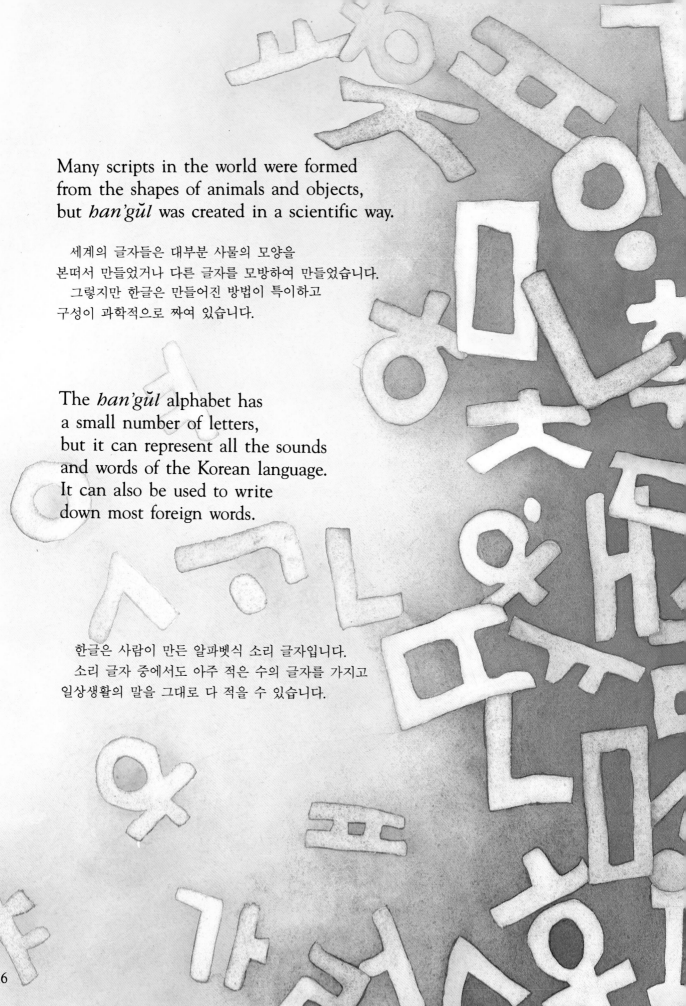

Many scripts in the world were formed
from the shapes of animals and objects,
but *han'gŭl* was created in a scientific way.

　세계의 글자들은 대부분 사물의 모양을
본떠서 만들었거나 다른 글자를 모방하여 만들었습니다.
　그렇지만 한글은 만들어진 방법이 특이하고
구성이 과학적으로 짜여 있습니다.

The *han'gŭl* alphabet has
a small number of letters,
but it can represent all the sounds
and words of the Korean language.
It can also be used to write
down most foreign words.

　한글은 사람이 만든 알파벳식 소리 글자입니다.
　소리 글자 중에서도 아주 적은 수의 글자를 가지고
일상생활의 말을 그대로 다 적을 수 있습니다.

16

Kim Sowol was a poet who sang about the natural beauty of his native land in unique Korean rhythm. He was a poet who planted warm human love and romance in the hearts of the Korean people.

Dear Mother, Dear Sister

by Kim Sowol

Dear mother, dear sister,
Let's live by the stream.
The bright, golden sands
Shining in the yard;
The song of reeds
Beyond the back gate.
Dear mother, dear sister,
Let's live by the stream.

엄마야 누나야 엄마야 누나야 강변 살자. / 뜰에는 반짝이는 금모래 빛 /
뒷문 밖에는 갈잎의 노래 / 엄마야 누나야 강변 살자.

17

Spring in My Native Village

고향의 봄

Words: Lee Won-su
Music: Hong Nan-p'a

Na - e - sa - al - dŏn Ko - hyang - ŭn Kkot - p'i - nŭn - sa - an Kkol -
나의 살던 고향은 꽃피는 산 - 골

Pok - sung - a - kkot Sal - gu - u - kkot A - gi - jin - da - al Rae -
복숭아꽃 살구 - 꽃 아기 진달 - 래

Spring in My Native Village

The native village where I lived
Is in the valley where flowers bloom,
A village, decorated like a Palace of Flowers,

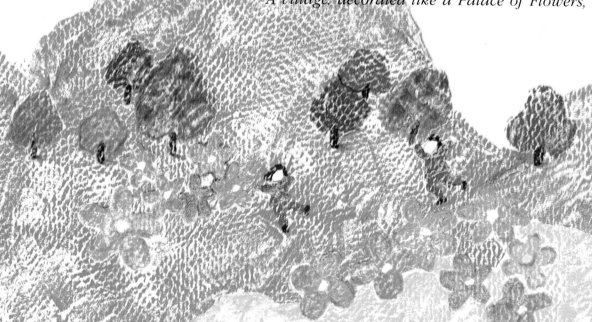

Ul - gŭt - bul - gŭt kko-ot-dae-gwol Ch'a-ri - in-do-ong Ne -
울 긋 불 긋 꽃 – 대 궐 차 린 – 동 – 네

Kŭ - so - ge - sŏ Nol-dŏ-ŏn-ttae-ga Kŭ-rip-sŭm-ni-i Ta -
그 속 에 서 놀 던 – 때 가 그 립 습 니 – 다

With multi-color blossoms
Of peach, apricot, and young azaleas.
I long for the days when I played amongst them.

The Faithful Daughter Shim Ch'ŏng

A long time ago, in the land by the Yellow Sea, there lived a goodhearted girl named Shim Ch'ŏng. She was raised by her blind father because her mother died three days after she was born.

Blind Shim carried his little daughter from house to house in search of women to give her milk.

In spite of all the hardships, Ch'ŏng grew into a strong, healthy girl.

Because Blind Shim was unable to work, Ch'ŏng had to do odd jobs in other people's homes from an early age so that she could provide her father with food and clothes.

Ch'ŏng was not only strong and healthy. She was also a very diligent worker. Everyone in the village praised her skill. Housewives even argued with each other over who would be next to get her to sew for them.

When Ch'ŏng was fifteen years old, something happened that changed her life forever. She went to a village far from home in order to work. There was so much work to do, it was dark before she was able to leave for home.

옛날 황해도 땅에 심 청이라는 아이가 살고 있었습니다.

태어난지 사흘만에 어머니가 돌아가신 불쌍한 청이는 앞 못 보는 아버지 손에 자랐습니다. 청이의 아버지 심 봉사는 어린 청이를 이집 저집 안고 다니며 동냥젖으로 키웠습니다. 그렇지만 청이는 아무 탈없이 무럭무럭 자랐습니다.

심 봉사는 앞을 볼 수가 없었기 때문에 아무 일도 하지 못했습니다. 그래서 청이는 어려서부터 남의 집일을 해주고 음식을 얻어와 아버지를 공양했습니다. 마을 사람들은 입을 모아 부지런하고 착한 청이를 칭찬했습니다. 청이는 아버지에게 좋은 음식과 옷을 지어드리기 위해 이른 아침부터 밤 늦게까지 열심히 일했습니다.

청이의 나이가 열다섯 살이 되던 해, 어느 날이었습니다.

It was very late at night and Blind Shim was very worried about Chŏng. "Where can the poor child be?" he asked himself. Then he went outside to wait for her.

He took his cane and fumbled across the bridge that led to the village. But he stumbled and fell plop into the stream below.

"Save me! Save me!" he shouted as he splashed about in the water.

A Buddhist monk was passing by just at that moment. He ran to the stream and pulled Blind Shim out of the water.

"Thank you, thank you," Blind Shim said over and over, as the monk led him back home.

"If you give Buddha 300 bags of rice," said the monk, "you will be able to see again." At this, Blind Shim perked up and he stopped saying, "Thank you, thank you." Instead he exclaimed, "What's that you said? I could see again?" Blind Shim was so excited at the possibility of seeing again that he made a promise without thinking. "Oh, holy monk," he said, "I will. I will give you 300 bags of rice."

After the monk left, Blind Shim began to think about the promise that he had made. He began to worry.

"How can I keep such a promise?" he asked himself. "Chŏng has a hard time just getting enough food for three small meals a day. How can she possibly get 300 bags of rice?"

When Chŏng finally got home, she saw her father's worried look. "Father," she asked, "what happened today?"

Blind Shim told her how he worried about her, how he fell into the stream, and how the monk saved him. And he told her he promised to give the monk 300 bags of rice in order to see again.

Chŏng tried to make her father feel better. "Don't worry," she said. "I will think of something."

건너 마을로 일을 나갔던 청이는 일이 많아서 밤 늦게까지 집으로 돌아올 수 없었습니다. 심 봉사는 걱정이 되어 청이를 마중하러 나섰습니다. 지팡이를 짚고 더듬거리며 마을 앞 다리를 건너던 심 봉사는 발을 헛디뎌 그만 개천에 '풍덩' 빠지고 말았습니다.

"아이쿠, 사람 살려! 사람 살려!" 심 봉사는 허위적거리며 소리를 질렀습니다.

때마침 그 곳을 지나던 스님이 얼른 달려와 심 봉사를 집으로 데려다 주었습니다.

"부처님께 쌀 삼백 석을 바치면 눈을 뜰 수 있지요." 심 봉사와 이야기를 나누던 스님은 이렇게 말했습니다.

"예! 눈을 뜰 수 있다구요?" 심 봉사는 귀가 번쩍 띄었습니다.

"스님, 쌀 삼백 석을 바치겠습니다." 심 봉사는 눈을 뜬다는 말에 생각할 겨를도 없이 덜컥 약속을 해버렸습니다. "내가 어쩌다 그런 약속을 했을까? 하루 세 끼 밥을 먹기도 어려운 살림인데……." 스님이 돌아가고나자 심 봉사는 걱정을 하기 시작했습니다. 늦게서야 집에 돌아온 청이는 이러한 심 봉사의 마음을 눈치챘습니다.

"아버지 제가 어떻게든 마련해 보겠어요. 너무 걱정하지 마세요." 청이는 아버지의 걱정을 덜어 주려고 이렇게 말했습니다.

For many days she thought about how she could ever get so many bags of rice. Then she heard that some sailors wanted to buy a young girl to sacrifice to the Dragon King so that they could make a safe journey.

Ch'ŏng went to the sailors and told them her sad story. She said she would sell herself to them for 300 bags of rice.

The sailors were very moved by her story, and very impressed by her goodheartedness. They told her, "Dear maiden, don't worry about your father any longer. We will give you the 300 bags of rice you need and we will also give your father rice to eat every day."

She tried to comfort her weeping father, but she had to leave him to go far away with the sailors.

At the sea coast they boarded a big ship and set sail for China. When the ship reached the middle of the Indangsu Sea, a strong wind suddenly began to blow and high waves rocked the ship.

The frightened sailors prepared a table of food offerings for the Dragon King. They bowed toward the sea and prayed, crying out, "Please. Please.

We beg you, great Dragon King. Spare us. Save us from this storm and let us cross the ocean."

Ch'ŏng stood at the front of the boat. She looked one last time in the direction of her home and then threw herself into the angry waves.

The sea suddenly became quiet. Relieved, but sad, the sailors sailed on. Several days passed.

Ch'ŏng had been asleep for a long time. She woke up and stretched her arms. "Where am I?" she asked herself.

She was in a beautiful room, the likes of which she had never seen before. Outside the windows, fish were swimming. A beautiful maiden came in and said, "Welcome to the Dragon Palace. The Dragon King brought you here when you sacrificed yourself to save the ship."

He knew how kindhearted Ch'ŏng was and how devoted she was to her father. So he put her inside the petals of a giant lotus flower and sent her back into the world.

Ch'ŏng slept peacefully inside the flower, gently rocking back and forth on the waves of the ocean.

Some fishermen saw the giant flower floating in the sea. "Oh!" they exclaimed, "Such a beautiful and magnificent flower must have been sent from the Dragon King." They pulled the lotus flower into their boat and took it to their king.

청이는 그렇게 많은 쌀을 어떻게 구해야 할지 여러 날을 곰곰이 생각해 보았습니다. 그러던 어느 날, 청이는 배를 타는 장사꾼들이 처녀를 사러 다닌다는 소문을 들었습니다. 청이는 장사꾼들을 찾아갔습니다. 장사꾼들은 아버지의 눈을 뜨게 하려는 청이의 고운 마음씨에 머리를 숙였습니다.

"아가씨, 이제 아버지 걱정은 하지 마시오. 쌀 삼백 석에다가 아버지가 먹고 살 수 있는 쌀을 더 드리겠소." 장사꾼들은 이렇게 약속을 했습니다.

청이는 불쌍한 아버지를 남겨 두고 장사꾼들을 따라 중국으로 떠나는 큰 배를 탔습니다. 배가 '인당수'라는 바다 가운데 이르자, 갑자기 사나운 바람이 불고 파도가 일었습니다. 그러자 장사꾼들은 상을 차려 놓고 바다를 향해 엎드려 빌기 시작했습니다.

"비나이다. 비나이다. 용왕님께 비나이다. 저희들이 살아서 바다를 건너게 해주십시오." 청이는 뱃머리에 서서 다시 한번 고향 쪽을 되돌아보고는 바다 속으로 풍덩 몸을 던졌습니다.

바다는 잔잔해졌습니다. 그리고 며칠이 지났습니다.

오랫동안 잠에 빠져 있던 청이는 기지개를 켜며 일어났습니다.

"아니, 여기가 어딜까?" 청이는 처음 보는 아름다운 방에 와 있었습니다.

창 밖에는 물고기들이 헤엄치고 있었습니다. 그 때 고운 여자 한 사람이 와서 말했습니다. "청이 아가씨, 이 곳은 바다 속의 용궁입니다.

용왕님께서 아가씨를 이 곳으로 데려오게 하셨지요."

용왕님은 효성이 지극한 청이를 커다란 연꽃 봉오리 속에 넣어 다시 세상으로 나가게 해주었습니다.

연꽃 속으로 들어간 청이는 바다 위로 두둥실 떠올랐습니다.

"이렇게 크고 아름다운 연꽃은 용왕님이 보내신 것이 틀림없어."

바다에서 고기를 잡던 어부들은 연꽃을 배에 싣고 가 임금님께 바쳤습니다.

The king also thought the huge lotus was a great wonder.

And then, all at once, the petals of the great lotus began to slowly open.

"What's this? Someone is coming out of the flower!"

In the middle of the lotus flower stood beautiful Chŏng. Everyone in the palace was very surprised, the king most of all. The king thought that the lotus maiden was so lovely that he asked her to become his queen.

Even after Chŏng became the queen, she still thought often about her poor blind father. At such times she became unbearably sad.

One day, when she was thinking of her home in the land by the Yellow Sea, the king asked her what was wrong. "If something is troubling you," he said, "please tell me." So Chŏng told him all about her life and about her father, Blind Shim.

After hearing Chŏng's sad story, the king slapped his knee and said, "I have it! We will hold a grand feast for all the blind people in the land. That way, we will be able to find your father."

The feast was held in the palace over many days. Every day, countless blind men were brought to the palace where they ate delicious food and were entertained by the court musicians. Queen Chŏng looked for her father every day. She looked and looked, but he didn't come.

The feast was almost over, and Ch'ŏng had almost given up hope, when an old blind man in very ragged clothes stumbled in.

"Father!" cried out the beautiful queen and she ran to the old man and hugged him.

Blind Shim's face was clouded in confusion.

"Who is this girl who calls me father?" he asked. When people told him it was the queen, he became even more confused.

"Father, it's me. Your daughter, Ch'ŏng," she said. Her father was so surprised that his eyes opened in amazement.

And he could see!

Blind Shim was not blind any more.

He shouted, "Oh! I see you at last!

I see my beautiful daughter at last!"

Shim Ch'ŏng and her father hugged each other tightly and cried tears of happiness.

임금님도 커다란 연꽃을 신기하게 여겼습니다. 그 때 연꽃 봉오리가 사르르 벌어졌습니다.

연꽃 속에는 아름다운 청이가 서 있었습니다. "아니! 연꽃에서 사람이 나오다니……." 사람들은 모두 깜짝 놀랐습니다. 임금님은 연꽃에서 나온 청이를 왕비로 맞아들였습니다.

그러나 왕비가 된 청이는 홀로 계신 아버지를 생각하며 늘 슬픔에 잠겨 있었습니다.

"걱정이 있으면 모두 이야기해 보시오." 그러자 청이는 지나간 이야기를 하기 시작했습니다.

"온 나라 안에 있는 장님들을 불러 모아 잔치를 베풀어 줍시다. 그러면 아버지를 찾을 수 있을 거요."

그 날부터 대궐에서는 큰 잔치가 베풀어졌습니다. 수많은 장님들이 대궐로 몰려들어와 맛있는 음식을 먹으며 즐겁게 놀았습니다. 청이는 이제나 저제나 아버지가 오시기를 애타게 기다렸습니다. 잔치가 끝나갈 무렵, 허름한 차림을 한 심 봉사가 더듬거리며 대궐 안으로 들어왔습니다.

"아버지!" 청이는 아버지를 와락 껴안았습니다.

"누구신데 나를 아버지라고 부르는 거요?" 심 봉사는 어리둥절하여 물었습니다.

"아버지, 저예요. 딸 청이에요."

"뭐라고, 내 딸 청이라고? 네가 살아 있었다니……, 어디 좀 보자." 심 봉사는 눈을 번쩍 떴습니다.

"아! 보이는구나. 내 딸 청이가 보이는구나!" 심 봉사는 청이를 얼싸안고 기쁨의 눈물을 흘렸습니다.

Children Enjoying Themselves in Winter

THROUGHOUT the year, Korean children enjoyed being outdoors. They seemed to enjoy winter more than any other season. They never tired of making snowmen and playing with snowballs. They also enjoyed sleighing and spinning tops on frozen streams. They did not feel the cold as they flew their kites, daring the winter wind to chase them into the house.

　한국의 어린이들은 자연 속에서 뛰어노는 것을 좋아했습니다. 추운 겨울에도 밖에서 신나게 놀았습니다. 눈사람 만들기나 눈싸움은 아무리 해도 싫증나지 않는 겨울철 놀이였습니다. 또 꽁꽁 얼어붙은 냇물에서 썰매를 타거나 팽이를 치는 것도 정말 즐거웠습니다. 겨울 바람을 맞으며 추위도 잊은 채 연을 날리는 아이도 있었습니다. 그들은 춥다고 집 안에만 있지는 않은 씩씩한 어린이들이었습니다.

Korea's Holidays

The first day of the first lunar month is Korea's ancient new year's day. Koreans call it Sŏllal. On that day, many people return to their native towns and villages to celebrate the new year's day with family members and offer thanks to their ancestors.

On new year's eve, they clean the entire house inside and out, and light candles throughout the night, and as they say farewell to the old year they wait for the arrival of the first day of the new year.

음력 1월 1일 새해 첫날, 설날입니다. 고향을 떠난 가족들은 모두가 고향을 찾아가서 가족들과 함께 설을 보내며 차례를 지냅니다.

설날 전날, 집 안 구석구석에 불을 밝히고 밤을 새우며, 묵은 해를 보내고 밝아오는 새해 첫날을 맞이합니다.

On the morning of new year's day, they put on new clothes and offer thanks to their ancestors. After that, the young ones bow to their elders, saying their new year's greetings. Next, they share the food and drink which was offered in a special ceremony to the spirits of their ancestors, as they remember the good things about their ancestors. On that day, everyone behaves well and prays for blessings in the new year.

설날 아침에는 미리 장만해 둔 설빔으로 갈아 입고 차례를 지냅니다. 차례가 끝나면 어른들께 세배를 합니다.

조상의 덕을 이어받는다는 생각에서 차례상에 올렸던 떡국과 음식과 술을 나눠 먹습니다. 설날은 새해 첫날인 만큼 행동을 함부로 하지 않고 새해 소망을 비는 날입니다.

The fifteenth day of the eighth lunar month is another happy holiday. It is called *Ch'usŏk* in Korean, which is Korea's Thanksgiving Day. The Koreans prepare food with new grain, bake Korean pastry called *songp'yŏn*, and buy fresh fruits to decorate the tables.

On that day, they offer thanks to the spirits of their ancestors for a good harvest. They visit the graves of their ancestors, and after cutting grass and pulling out the weeds around the grave-mounds, they again offer thanks to the spirits of their ancestors.

음력 8월 15일, 추석입니다.
햇곡식으로 음식을 마련하고 송편을 빚고 햇과일을 준비합니다. 그리고 일 년 동안 농사를 잘 짓게 되었음을 조상님께 감사드립니다. 산소에 찾아가 벌초를 하고 성묘도 합니다.

The day is a joyful one as they share many delicious foods and fruits. They also realize that *Ch'usŏk* is a silent reminder of the ancestors that one must not forget the good deeds and kindness of others.

여러 가지 햇과일과 음식을 나누어 먹으면서 즐겁게 보냅니다. 무엇보다도 추석은 부모, 조상, 친지의 고마움을 잊지 말라는 조상들의 말없는 가르침이기도 합니다.

Messenger from the Mountain Spirit

ANCIENT Koreans revered nature and believed spirits inhabited inanimate objects such as rocks, trees and mountains. They thought that the tiger was the messenger of the Spirit of the Mountain and thus a bearer of good fortune. They also thought that a picture of a tiger would protect the house from evil spirits.

예로부터 한국 사람들은 자연을 숭상하고, 그것에 영혼이 있다고 믿었습니다. 호랑이는 그들에게 '산신의 사자', '행운의 전령' 이었으며, 호랑이의 그림은 집 안의 잡귀를 쫓는 데 사용 되었습니다.

The Civilized Koreans

What kind of life did the Koreans have? They worked hard as they formed villages and plowed the fields in the land of mild climate with many mountains and clean streams and rivers, of blue skies and four distinctive seasons.

Old Chinese records tell us many things about the life of the people in this land of beauty called *kŭmsu kangsan*, which means "the rivers and mountains embroidered on silk." A Chinese record says that "The Koreans love singing and dancing." Another Chinese record says that they were good-humored, civilized, and polite. It says that "They avoid quarrels and love peace. However, they are brave, and when they are mistreated they would not hesitate to fight to death."

The Koreans fought wars against others only to defend their country and not for other people's territory. They wanted to be strong by having an advanced culture rather than by taking other people's lands by force to satisfy their greed.

The Koreans lived in a small peninsular nation and they developed an advanced culture with peace-loving hearts.

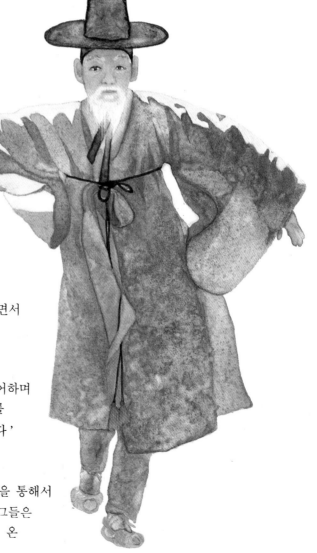

산이 많고 풍부한 물과 맑은 하늘을 안고 사계절이 뚜렷한
온대 지방. 이 곳에서 마을을 이루고 오손도손 논과 밭을 갈면서
살아온 한국 사람들의 생활모습은 어떠할까요?
　중국의 옛 책들에 기록된 것을 보면
'금수강산'에 사는 사람들의 모습을 잘 말하고 있습니다.
　'한국 민족은 온유하고 양보하기를 좋아하고 다투기를 싫어하며
　천성이 선량하였고 평화를 사랑하였다. 그러나 일단 불의를
　당했을 경우에는 생명을 아끼지 않는 용맹한 성품을 지녔다'
는 것입니다. 한국 사람들이 다른 나라와 싸운 것은 남을
침략하기 위해서가 아니라 나라를 보호하려는 것이었습니다.
　힘으로 남의 땅을 빼앗아 만족해하기보다는 오직 문화예술을 통해서
강해지고 싶어했습니다. 반도에 치우친 조그만 나라, 한국. 그들은
평화를 사랑하는 마음으로 세계가 부러워하는 문화를 이룩해 온
사람들입니다.

CH'ŎMSŎNGDAE (Star Observation Tower)

CH'ŎMSŎNGDAE is one of the oldest and the largest observatories in Asia. It was built some 1,300 years ago to calculate the movements of the stars, observe the appearance of comets, and record eclipses of the sun and the moon.

동양에서 가장 크고 오래된 천문대입니다. 1300년 전, 하늘을 관측하기 위해 경주에 세운 것입니다. 첨성대에서 별자리의 움직임과 혜성의 출현을 살폈고 일식과 월식을 관측하였습니다.

SŎKKURAM (Stone Grotto Temple)

SŎKKURAM is a man-made stone grotto Buddhist temple built on the high slope of a mountain near Kyŏngju. It has a rectangular front room and a round inner chamber with a domed ceiling formed with carefully cut blocks of stone. A large stone statue of Buddha is placed in the center of the inner chamber, and there are many images of Buddha carved on the stone walls of the front room. The grotto temple and statues of Buddha are beautiful art works of the ancient Korean sculptors.

자연의 거대한 바위덩어리를 뚫어서 방을 만들었습니다. 아치형으로 돌을 쌓아 천장을 만들었으며, 그 가운데 돌로 된 부처와 그 둘레에 새겨진 여러 불상은 서로 아름답게 조화되어 예술의 극치를 이루고 있습니다.

PULGUKSA (The Pulguk Temple)

PULGUKSA is a large Buddhist temple which was constructed some 1,200 years ago. It was built during a period of some thirty years from 751 by a Buddhist named Kim Tae-sŏng. He constructed this temple for the well-being of his own parents as well as his country and countrymen. This temple, located in Kyŏngju, has been designated by the Korean government as Historic and Scenic Place No. 1.

불국사는 석굴암과 함께 지금으로부터 1200여년 전 김대성이라는 사람이 자신의 부모와 나라의 안정 등 모든 사람들이 행복해지기를 비는 마음으로 30년의 세월 동안 지은 큰 절입니다. 불국사는 역사적인 명승 제1호로 한국 불교미술의 절정을 이룬 보물입니다.

CH'ŎNGJA (Green Celadon)

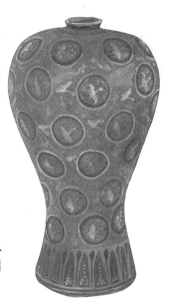

KOREANS are genteel people who love clean colors. The color of the green celadon that Koreans call *ch'ŏngja* represents the Korean mind.

Celadon is superior to most other porcelain wares. It is so because of its shape, line, color, design, and the unique inlaying technique called *sanggam*.

It is a world-class artistic product which represents the creative and refined cultural life of the Korean people.

한국 사람들은 언제나 하늘같이 파랗고 그윽했습니다. 청자가 지닌 빛깔은 바로 한국인의 마음입니다. 청자는 그릇의 모양과 선, 색, 무늬, 독특한 상감법 등에서 다른 나라의 자기보다 우수하며, 한국인의 창의력과 세련된 문화생활을 보여 주는 세계적인 예술품입니다.

The Tripitaka Koreana

THE *Tripitaka* ("Three Baskets") is a complete collection of the sacred teachings of Buddhism. In 1251, the *Tripitaka Koreana*, known in Korean as Koryŏ Taejanggyŏng, was printed with 81,113 wood blocks as an offering of prayer to Buddha for the safety of the nation and well-being of the people at the time when the Mongols invaded Korea.

It took sixteen long years to carve these wood blocks. Each block was first soaked in sea water and then steamed before letters were carved on it.

Because of the fine carving, and also because of the fact that no block had any poorly carved letters, it is regarded as a unique cultural property of the world.

대장경은 나무를 바닷물에 담갔다가 쪄서 말린 다음, 한 자씩 판에 새긴 불경으로, 나라와 국민들이 편안하기를 부처님께 비는 마음과 정성이 담겨져 있습니다. 경판이 81,113장으로 이루어진 팔만대장경은, 만드는데 16년이라는 긴 세월이 걸렸습니다. 또한 새겨진 글자체가 매우 아름답고, 틀린 글자가 없다는 점에서 세계적인 문화재로 인정받고 있습니다.

Metal Type

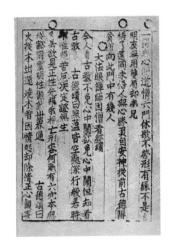

IN 1234 Korea was the first country to publish books with metal type. It was not until 200 years later that books were published in the West with metal type. The first book published with metal type in Korea was entitled *The Handbook for King's Secret Inspectors*. The only surviving copy of this book is currently preserved in the Paris National Library.

한국은 세계에서 가장 먼저 금속활자를 이용하여 책을 만들어 냈습니다 (1234). 이것은 서양의 활자 인쇄기술보다 약 200년이나 앞선 것입니다. 현재, 파리 국립도서관에 보관된 '직지심경'은 이 세상에 남아 있는 가장 오래된 금속활자 인쇄본입니다.

The Community of Hwarang

Some 1,400 years ago, the king and his ministers of the Shilla kingdom were worried when they could not find well-qualified and good people who could serve the nation in the government. They therefore adopted a plan to organize the people and let them live together so that they could carefully watch their behavior and select good men among them.

The king believed that to make the country peaceful, strong, and prosperous, he needed many young people who were obedient and loyal, so he selected handsome, healthy, and well-mannered young men and organized them into the group. These young men were called *hwarang*, which means "flowery youths" in Korean. They were sons of aristocratic families.

These *hwarang* increased their knowledge and sang songs, and they encouraged each other to be good. They visited many famous, sacred mountains and rivers, purifying their minds and training their bodies. By doing these things they came to know what was right and what was wrong, and what was good and what was bad. Many members of the Community of Hwarang became wise and loyal ministers, as well as brave and good warriors.

Under the leadership of their leaders, the members of the Community of Hwarang became loyal to the king, kind and obedient to their parents, and patriotic to their country. They developed strong friendship among themselves based on trust.

Although they became courageous fighters in the battlefields, they learned that they must value human life, and never kill people indiscriminately. They developed a strong warrior spirit and military art as they trained their minds and bodies. Yet they enjoyed singing and dancing in the woods. When the country was in danger, they went to war and gave their lives to save it. They were the pillars of the state and the protectors of the kingdom.

Such patriotic spirit of the *hwarang* has survived, and whenever the country faces danger, brave soldiers come forward.

지금으로부터 약 1400년 전입니다. 임금님과 신하들은 나라에 필요한 인재를 알아보지 못하여 걱정을 하고 있었습니다. 훌륭한 사람을 알아 내고 뽑는 방법을 여러 가지로 궁리한 끝에 많은 사람들을 함께 모여 지내도록 하였습니다. 그리고 그들의 행동을 자세히 살핀 후에 인재를 뽑아 보기로 하였습니다.

임금은 나라를 화평하게 하자면 효도하고 충성할 줄 아는 젊은이들이 많이 있어야겠다고 여겼습니다. 그리하여 전국에서 덕행이 있고 아름답게 생긴 소년을 뽑아 '화랑'이라 부르고 이 화랑을 중심으로 낭도들을 모았습니다.

낭도들은 지식을 쌓고 노래를 부르며 서로 격려하였습니다. 또한 유명한 산과 강을 찾아다니며 몸과 마음을 깨끗이 하였습니다. 이렇게 함으로써 세상의 옳고 그름을 가릴 줄 아는 사람들이 되었습니다. 어질고 충성스런 신하가 화랑도에서 나왔습니다. 용감하고 선량한 군사들도 생겨나게 되었습니다.

지도자인 화랑과 그를 따르는 낭도들로 구성된 화랑도는 나라에 충성하고, 부모에 효도하며, 믿음으로 친구를 사귀고, 싸움터에 나가서는 물러섬이 없으며, 함부로 살생하지 않도록 배웠습니다. 이렇게 자란 청소년들은 나라의 튼튼한 기둥이 되었습니다. 그들은 평소에 아름다운 숲 속에서 노래와 춤을 즐기며 무술을 익혀 몸과 마음을 다스렸습니다. 그리고 나라가 위태로워졌을 때는 전쟁터에 나아가 목숨을 바쳐 나라를 지켰습니다. 한국의 옛 사회에서 볼 수 있었던 화랑의 무사도 정신은 사라지지 않고 면면히 이어내려와 국난을 맞을 때는 의병 등의 의기로 치솟곤 했습니다.

T'aekwondo, the Korean Martial Art

T'AEKWONDO is a unique Korean martial art. It is an art of self-defense by attacking the opponent with various movements of clenched fists, open hand, or foot. It is a very popular sport among Korean children and young people because through it one can develop the right state of mind and strengthen the body.

태권도는 한국의 독특한 무예입니다. 맨손과 맨주먹으로 찌르고, 치고, 발로 차서, 상대방을 공격하여 자기 몸을 방어합니다. 태권도는 몸을 튼튼하게 해주며 올바른 정신을 길러주는 건전한 스포츠이므로 한국의 어린이들과 청소년들에게 매우 인기있는 운동 중의 하나입니다.

Ssirŭm, Korean Wrestling

IN Korea, wrestling is a traditional, competitive sport. Facing each other, two opponents grip a belt that is loosely wound around the waist and legs. The first person to throw the other to the ground is the winner. Traditionally, the winner of the final bout was awarded a bull, a considerably valuable prize at that time. In addition, he was given the title "the strongest man under heaven." The competitive rules in wrestling emphasize gentlemanly conduct and sportsmanship.

씨름은 한국의 남성들 사이에서 오래 전부터 행하여 오던 가장 대중적인 경기입니다. 두 사람이 서로 붙잡고 힘과 기술로 상대방을 먼저 바닥에 넘어뜨리는 것입니다. 경기의 우승자에게는 황소 한 마리를 상품으로 주기도 했는데, 그 승리자를 장사라고 부릅니다.

The Tiger and the Dried Persimmon

Once upon a time, in a valley deep in the mountains, there lived a huge tiger. He always walked around and boasted about his great strength, saying, "I dare anyone to match my strength." When the other animals on the mountain heard him, they all shrieked and ran away.

There was a very cold winter one year. The snow piled up over many days, so the tiger could not dig out of his cave.

"I'm so hungry I can't stand it any longer," he grumbled, and he slowly and painfully got out of his cave.

The thick snow made the entire mountain white.

"Oh, no!" the tiger mumbled. "Even though I'm very hungry, there's nothing to eat!" As he wandered around the mountains, every few footsteps he sank deep down into the snow.

By the time darkness fell, the tiger had reached the village which lay at the foot of the mountain. He snooped and poked around until he found a barn outside a farmhouse. A fat cow was asleep inside, snoring loudly.
"A cow!" exclaimed the tiger.

"That should make a good meal!" he said, licking his chops.

But just at that moment, the tiger heard a small child crying inside the house. "Waa! Waa!" "Eh! What's that noise?" thought the tiger.

He sneaked up to the room in which the child was crying.

까마득한 옛날, 깊은 산골짜기에 커다란 호랑이 한 마리가 살고 있었습니다. 호랑이는 자기가 힘이 세다는 것을 크게 뽐내고 다녔습니다.

"나보다 힘센 놈이 있으면 어디 나와 봐라." 호랑이는 이렇게 말하며 온 산이 쩌렁쩌렁 울리도록 '어홍'하고 울부짖었습니다. 산 속의 작은 짐승들은 그 소리에 놀라 허둥지둥 도망치기에 바빴습니다.

어느 해 추운 겨울이었습니다. 며칠 동안 눈이 펑펑 쏟아져서 호랑이는 동굴 밖으로 나갈 수가 없었습니다. "이거 배가 고파 더는 못 견디겠는데……." 호랑이는 어슬렁어슬렁 먹이를 찾아 나섰습니다.

"아이구, 배 고파. 아무것도 먹을 것이 없잖아." 호랑이는 눈 속에 푹푹 빠지면서 산 속을 돌아 다녔습니다.   날이 저물자, 호랑이는 산 아래 있는 마을로 내려갔습니다.

이집 저집을 기웃거리던 호랑이는 어느 농부의 집 외양간을 찾아냈습니다.   외양간 안에는 살찐 소 한 마리가 쿨쿨 잠을 자고 있었습니다.

"옳지, 소라도 잡아먹어야 겠다 !" 호랑이는 군침을 꿀꺽 삼켰습니다.

38

In the room, the child's mother was trying to make the child stop crying.

The mother said, "Oh look! There's a monster! You had better stop crying or he'll come here and get you!"

But the baby kept crying.

So the mother said, "There's a tiger outside! If you keep crying, he'll come and eat you!" She had not really seen the tiger. She was only trying to scare her child to make him stop crying.

But when the tiger heard this, he thought that the mother had seen him.

"How can she know I am here?" he wondered. "I must be more careful."

The baby cried even louder. "What's this?" thought the tiger. He didn't like the idea of a baby not being afraid of a tiger.

그 때 집 안에서 '응아응아'하는 아기의 울음소리가 들렸습니다. '이크! 이게 무슨 소리지?'

호랑이는 살금살금 방으로 다가가 보았습니다. 방에서는 아기엄마가 우는 아기를 달래고 있었습니다.

"아가, 도깨비가 왔다. 어서 그쳐야지." 아기는 계속 울어댔습니다.

"저기 좀 봐! 밖에 호랑이가 왔다. 아이 무서워!"

아기엄마는 진짜 호랑이가 온 것을 보지는 못했지만 아기를 달래기 위해 이렇게 말했습니다.

그 말을 들은 호랑이는 덜컥 겁이 났습니다. '저 아기엄마는 내가 온 걸 어떻게 알았을까!'

아기는 더 큰 소리로 울었습니다.

'아니, 저 아이는 내가 하나도 무섭지 않은 모양이구나!'

The child cried and cried. Nothing could scare the child into silence. Finally, the mother tried something different. She reached into a cabinet and pulled out something the child could eat. "Look! Here is a dried persimmon!" she said. The child immediately stopped crying and started eating the persimmon.

The tiger, who had been listening to all of this from outside the room, was very surprised. Of course, he hadn't seen what had happened inside the room. "A persimmon?" He thought and thought. "A persimmon must be a very scary beast since it stopped that child from crying. It must be more powerful and frightening than I am, since I didn't scare the child at all. If I dawdle around here very long, the persimmon might eat me!"

The tiger walked very carefully back to the barn.

It was very dark inside the barn. At that moment, a big black thing crept through the barn door. "Oh, no! That thing must be the persimmon!" thought the tiger.

The tiger was so scared it couldn't move. The black shape walked with big strides up to where the tiger was sitting. It reached down and, very gently, it rubbed its hand across the tiger's back. Then it said, "This one's really nice and fat!"

The tiger was so scared that it just stood there shaking.

아기가 계속 울어대자, 아기엄마는 벽장을 부시럭부시럭 뒤져서 무엇인가를 꺼내 왔습니다.
"아가야. 곶감이다." 그러자 아기는 울음을 뚝 그쳤습니다.
바깥에서 듣고 있던 호랑이는 깜짝 놀랐습니다. '곶감? 곶감이 대체 어떻게 생긴 놈이길래 저 아기가 울음을 그쳤을까? 나보다 힘이 세고 무서운 놈인 것이 틀림없어. 여기서 꾸물거리다가는 잡아먹히 겠는걸!' 호랑이는 슬슬 뒷걸음질을 쳐서 외양간으로 들어갔습니다. 외양간은 아주 어두웠습니다. 그 때 외양간 안으로 웬 시커먼 것이 불쑥 들어왔습니다.
'이크, 저놈이 바로 곶감이구나!'
호랑이는 무서워서 꼼짝도 못하고 서 있었습니다. 시커먼 것은 성큼성큼 호랑이에게로 다가왔습니다. 그리고 호랑이의 등을 슬슬 쓰다듬으며 말했습니다.
"그놈 참 살도 포동포동하게 쪘네."
호랑이는 겁에 질려서 부들부들 떨었습니다.

The big black thing that the tiger thought was a persimmon was really a thief who had come to steal the farmer's cow.

But it was dark and the thief couldn't see very well inside the barn.

He thought the furry tiger was the cow. So the thief gently led the tiger outside. Once outside the barn, the thief reached down and patted the tiger again, but this time he noticed that the fur he touched wasn't cow fur. He looked down and thought, "Oh, no! This isn't a cow at all. It's a tiger!" The thief was so surprised.

The tiger, on the other hand, thought that the persimmon had gotten him for sure.

He closed his eyes and thought, "Oh, no! The ferocious persimmon is surely going to eat me!"

호랑이가 곶감이라고 생각한 것은 소를 훔치러 온 도둑이었습니다.
소도둑은 외양간이 너무 어두워서 안을 잘 볼 수가 없었습니다.
소도둑은 부드러운 털의 호랑이가 소일 거라고 생각했습니다.
소도둑은 호랑이를 살살 끌고 외양간을 나왔습니다. 그리고 다시 한번 호랑이를 쓰다듬다가 깜짝 놀랐습니다.
'이크, 이건 호랑이 아니야!'
소도둑은 너무 놀라서 소리를 지를 뻔했습니다.
한편, 호랑이는 호랑이대로 확실히 자신이 곶감에게 잡혔다고 생각했습니다. '이제 곶감이란 놈에게 잡아먹히는구나!'
호랑이는 두 눈을 딱 감았습니다.

The thief was too afraid to move, so he just stood still next to the tiger.

The tiger thought, "This is my chance!"

And he jumped free and tried to run away.

But when the thief felt the tiger start to move, he thought that the tiger was going to try to grab and eat him.

So he immediately jumped onto the tiger's back and held on for dear life.

The scared tiger leaped up and down and ran around in circles trying to throw the thief off his back.

But this only made the thief hold on even tighter.

The tiger then ran wildly, thinking, "No matter how strong a persimmon is, it will surely fall off when I run as fast as I can."
So the tiger used all of his strength to run as fast as an arrow.

The tiger, with the thief on his back, quickly ran out of the village and turned onto a mountain path.

소도둑은 옴짝달싹 못 하고 호랑이 옆에 서 있었습니다.

'옳지, 이 때다!'

호랑이는 소도둑이 머뭇거리는 틈을 타서 도망을 가려고 했습니다.

소도둑은 호랑이가 움직이자 자기를 잡아먹으려는 줄 알고, 얼른 호랑이 등에 올라가 힘껏 깍지를 꼈습니다. 호랑이는 겁이 나서 껑충껑충 뛰었습니다.

소도둑은 떨어지지 않으려고 호랑이의 등을 더욱 꽉 붙잡았습니다.

호랑이는 소도둑을 떨어뜨리려고 펄쩍펄쩍 뛰기도 하고 뱅글뱅글 맴을 돌기도 했습니다.

소도둑은 호랑이 등을 더 단단히 붙잡았습니다.

그러자 호랑이는 마구 달리기 시작했습니다.

'이렇게 빨리 달리면 아무리 무서운 곶감이라도 떨어지고 말겠지?'

호랑이는 있는 힘을 다하여 쏜살같이 달렸습니다.

호랑이와 소도둑은 마을을 벗어나 산길로 접어들었습니다.

Dawn came and the day grew bright.

The thief looked above his head and saw a branch of a tree hanging down. He reached up and grabbed the branch. He held the branch tightly and the tiger ran out from beneath him.

But the tiger kept running and didn't look back. He was so scared and tired that he didn't even notice the thief was gone at first. After he ran a while longer, though, he noticed that his back felt lighter, so he stopped running and heaved a great sigh of relief.

이윽고 날이 밝기 시작했습니다.

호랑이 등에 찰싹 달라붙어 있던 소도둑은 머리 위에 나뭇가지들이 드리워져 있는 것을 보았습니다.

소도둑은 얼른 손을 뻗쳐 큰 나뭇가지에 대롱대롱 매달렸습니다.

그래도 호랑이는 뒤도 돌아보지 않고 계속 달렸습니다.

한참을 달리다가 등이 가벼워진 것을 안 호랑이는 크게 한숨을 쉬며 털썩 주저앉았습니다.

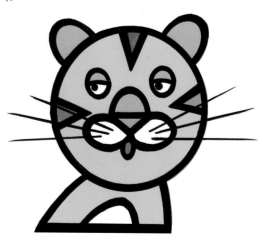

**"Whew!" he sighed.
"That was close!
Today I was nearly eaten by a persimmon."**

"휴우, 하마터면 곶감이란 놈에게 잡아먹힐 뻔했네."

A Father and Three Sons

Long, long ago, there lived a father and three sons. All three sons were talented, and they were serious and hard-working. But sadly, there was no love between them, and they did not like to help each other or work together, perhaps because each had too much faith in himself.

One day, the father called his three sons together, and said:

"Break this tree branch here."

The three sons smiled mockingly as if to say: "That's too easy," and each of them broke the branch without any trouble.

Next, the father said:

"Hold three branches together, and break them."

Each of the three sons held three branches together, and tried with all his might to break them but could not.

Then, the father said to them:

"You see, one branch is easy to break no matter how strong it may be when it is alone. But if their strength is combined no one can break them."

The three sons understood the meaning of these wise words of their father. After that, they helped each other and grew up to be fine men.

옛날에 아버지와 세 명의 아들이 함께 살고 있었습니다.

세 명의 아들은 모두 재능이 뛰어나고 성실하였습니다. 그러나 그 아들들은 자신의 능력을 믿어서인지 형제 간의 우애도 없고 힘을 모아 무슨 일을 하는 것을 몹시 싫어했습니다.

어느 날, 아버지는 세 명의 아들을 한자리에 모이게 하였습니다.

"자, 여기에 있는 나뭇가지를 한번 부러뜨려 보아라." 세 아들은 너무 쉬운 일을 시킨다는 듯 피식 웃더니 단숨에 그 나뭇가지를 부러뜨렸습니다.

"그러면 이 세 개의 나뭇가지를 한꺼번에 쥐고 부러뜨려 보아라." 세 아들은 모두가 힘을 써 보았지만 도저히 그것을 부러뜨릴 수가 없었습니다.

"그것 보아라. 아무리 강하고 잘난 나뭇가지도 저 하나만 뽑낼 때에는 이렇듯 힘없이 부러지고 만다. 하지만 그것들이 힘을 합하면 그 누구도 부러뜨리지 못하는 것이 된단다."

세 아들은 아버지의 말씀에 크게 깨닫고 다음부터는 서로 돕고 힘을 합하여 모두 훌륭하게 자랐다고 합니다.

The Village Where Apricot Flowers Bloom

A poem by Lee Ho-u

Wherever apricot flowers bloom
Seems like my native village.

Whomever I meet there
I wish to pat their backs.

Who would not welcome me
If I dropped into their homes?

살구꽃 핀 마을 살구꽃 핀 마을은 어디나 고향 같다. / 만나는 사람마다 등이라도 치고지고 /
뉘 집을 들어서 본들 반겨 아니 맞으리.

Farm Villages in Autumn

KOREAN farm villages are most beautiful in autumn.
The skies are blue and high in this season.
The fields are golden with ripe grain,
and persimmon trees are laden with fruit.
All is beautiful in this season.

한국의 농촌이 가장 아름다울 때는 가을입니다.
맑고 깨끗한 하늘은 푸르고 높습니다.
곡식이 무르익은 들판은
황금빛으로 물들며, 온갖 것들이 풍요롭습니다.

King Sejong

Sejong was a Korean king who lived some 590 years ago. King Sejong loved the people and served them well. He enjoyed reading books, and even as a young boy, was interested in learning. The lamp in his room was always lit until late at night.

Sejong built a center for learning known as the Hall for the Assembly of Wise Persons (Chiphyŏnjŏn) for the purpose of promoting scholarship and developing culture. He brought together at this hall wise and talented men, encouraged them to study, and provided them with much help. He often visited the hall after reading books until late at night, and he enjoyed discussing ideas with them.

King Sejong was also keenly interested in science and astronomy. He sought out talented scientists, and with his support they invented such items as sun dials, water clocks, and rain gauges. In fact the rain gauge was invented by the Korean scientists, who were the members of the Hall for the Assembly of Wise Persons, some 200 years earlier than the one which Castelli of Italy invented. After the invention of the rain gauge, many others were produced and they were installed throughout the kingdom, measuring rainfall in various parts of the country accurately. Korean farmers were helped greatly by knowing the amount of rainfall in each season. Meanwhile, King Sejong encouraged the creation of better metal type and as a result many books were published. In such ways, he contributed toward cultural progress and helped the people to improve their livelihood with the help of many honest and upright ministers. Along with those scholars at the Hall for the Assembly of Wise Persons, he advanced benevolent rule and promoted the national culture of Korea.

옛날, 국민을 자식처럼 아끼고 사랑한 세종이라는 인자한 임금이 있었습니다. 그는 어려서부터 책 읽기를 좋아하고 학문을 사랑하였습니다.

세종은 '인재를 길러내는 슬기의 집'이라는 집현전을 세워서, 성품이 어질고 학식이 높은 학자들을 모아 마음껏 연구를 하도록 뒷바침해 주었습니다.

세종은 밤 늦게까지 책을 보다가 집현전에 나가 집현전 학자들과 이야기 나누기를 무척 즐겼습니다. 뿐만 아니라 과학과 천문기상에 대해서도 깊은 관심을 갖고 장영실, 이 천 등과 같은 재능있는 과학자들과 함께 해시계·물시계·간의·측우기 등을 만들어 냈습니다. 무엇보다도 측우기는 이탈리아의 카스텔리가 만든 것보다 약 200년이나 앞선 세계 최초의 발명품입니다. 측우기로 비가 내리는 양을 과학적으로 알아내자 농사를 보다 효율적으로 짓게 되었습니다.

King Sejong always regretted that Korea had no written language of its own, although it had its own spoken language. He also regretted the fact that many people could not submit written petitions to the government because they did not know how to write Chinese characters. It must be remembered that all public documents, including people's petitions, were written in Chinese at that time. So, King Sejong commissioned the scholars at the Hall for the Assembly of Wise Persons to invent a suitable and appropriate Korean alphabet. He himself showed keen interest in creating a Korean writing system.

Finally, in 1443 the Korean alphabet of twenty-eight letters was invented. It was the fruit of the long, hard work of his scholars. Before adopting it as an official Korean alphabet, King Sejong used it to compile a book, and in 1446 it was officially adopted. He called it *Hunmin jŏng'ŭm*, which means "Correct Sounds to Instruct the People." It is commonly called *han'gŭl*.

Today, about 550 years later, Koreans are still using this alphabet, which is regarded as the most unique and scientific one in the world.

In 1450, King Sejong died at the age of fifty-four. He was an outstanding king whose glorious life was dedicated to the well-being of the nation and the people, as well as to the advancement of scholarship and science. He is remembered as Sejong the Great, and his birth and deeds are celebrated each year on *Han'gŭl* Day, which is October 9th.

한편 세종은 활자를 더욱 정교하게 만들어 생활에 필요한 많은 책들을 간행하기도 하였습니다. 이렇듯 국민을 위하고 문화의 발전에 힘쓴 세종에게는 인품이 원만하고 생활이 청렴한 황 희·맹사성과 같은 훌륭한 명신들이 따르고 있었습니다. 또한 집현전 학자들의 노력과 뛰어난 재능이 함께 어우러져 정치와 문화를 발전시켜 나가는데 어려움이 없었습니다.

세종은 한국말을 기록할 한국 고유의 글자가 없음을 언제나 안타깝게 여겼습니다. 그리하여 집현전 학자들로 하여금 한국말을 적는데 가장 알맞은 글자를 만들도록 하고 이를 위하여 온갖 힘을 다하였습니다.

누구보다도 그 자신이 이 연구에 깊은 관심을 가지고 정열을 쏟았으며, 글자의 기초가 되는 이론을 연구하는 데 많은 노력을 기울였습니다.

1443년 닿소리 열일곱 자, 홀소리 열한 자로 된 한글이 만들어졌습니다. 이것은 실로 피땀어린 연구와 노력의 결정이었습니다.

세종은 새 글자의 실용성을 알아보기 위하여 이 글자들을 이용해서 '용비어천가'라는 책을 만들게 하였습니다.

그 후, 1446년 드디어 한국의 자랑스러운 새 글자, 한글이 세상에 반포되었습니다. 그로부터 약 550년이 지난 오늘날에도 한국 사람들은 한글을 사용하고 있으며, 한글은 독창적이고 과학적인 글자로 세계에서 인정받고 있습니다. 1450년 세종은 쉰넷의 생애를 마치기까지 오로지 나라와 백성을 위해 정치를 한 훌륭한 왕이었습니다.

The Ogres' Magic Clubs

A long time ago, a kindhearted young man lived in a small village. One day, he went to the mountains to gather some wood. He worked hard to gather together a big load. After he finished, he sat in the shade and wiped the sweat from his face. At that moment, he felt something hit him on the head.

"Ouch! What is this? Ah, it's a hazelnut. I'll give it to my father," he decided, and put it in his pocket.

Clunk! Another hazelnut fell on his head.

Then he thought, "I'll give this one to my mother." And he put it in his pocket, too.

Clunk! Clunk! This time, two hazelnuts fell together.

"Wow!" exclaimed the young man. "This is my lucky day! These two nuts are for my older brother and me."

Soon, the sun started to set behind the mountain and it became very dark. To make matters worse, big, thick drops of rain started to fall.

The young man quickly picked up the load of wood and put it on his shoulders. The raindrops became even bigger.

옛날, 어느 마을에 욕심 많은 형과 마음씨 착한 아우가 살았습니다.

어느 날, 아우는 나무를 하러 산으로 올라갔습니다. 아우는 나무를 한 짐 해놓고, 나무그늘에 앉아 땀을 식혔습니다. 그 때 무언가가 머리를 '딱' 때리고 떨어졌습니다.

"아야! 이게 뭐지? 어, 개암이로구나. 아버지께 갖다 드려야겠다." 아우는 개암을 주웠습니다.

"투둑투둑" 이번에는 개암 여러 개가 한꺼번에 떨어졌습니다.

"야! 오늘은 재수가 좋은 날이구나. 이건 어머니 갖다 드려야지. 또 이건 형님하고 내가 먹어야지."
아우는 개암을 주워서 주머니에 넣었습니다.

어느 새 해가 뉘엿뉘엿 넘어갔습니다.

그런데 갑자기 굵은 빗방울이 후둑후둑 떨어지기 시작했습니다.

아우는 얼른 나뭇짐을 챙겼습니다. '쏴아' 빗줄기는 더욱 굵어졌습니다.

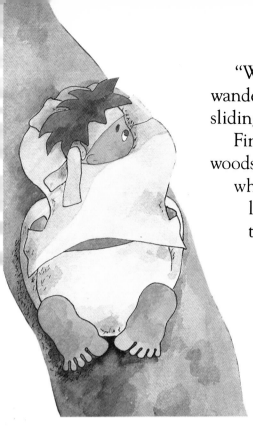

"Where can I get out of this rain?" he wondered as he wandered around the mountains, his feet slipping and sliding on the wet leaves.

Finally, he came to a small cottage hidden in the woods. "Whew! At last I've found a place to rest for a while," he thought and quickly went inside. The place looked like it had not been lived in for a long, long time. But it wasn't long before he heard something. It was the thump, thump, thump of big footsteps. The young man shook with fear. "What kind of people would live here? They must be thieves!" he thought, looking for a place to hide.

He quickly climbed up onto a beam high above the floor. A group of figures burst into the dark cottage, laughing, "A-ho-ho-ho, a-hee-hee-hee...."

When he looked down and saw them, the young man was so surprised that he almost fell off the beam. They were not people at all! They were a bunch of ogres, with horns on their heads.

The young man shook with fright, even more than he had before.

Then one of the ogres shouted, "Well, shall we begin our game?"

Thump! Thwack! The ogres struck the floor with their clubs as they sang:

"어디 비를 피할 곳이 없을까?" 아우는 젖은 풀잎에 쭈루룩쭈루룩 미끄러지면서 산길을 헤맸습니다. 그러다가 조그만 외딴집을 찾아냈습니다. "휴우, 잘 됐다. 저기서 좀 쉬었다 가자."
아우는 얼른 집 안으로 들어갔습니다. 그런데 조금 뒤에 '쿵쾅쿵쾅'하는 커다란 발자국 소리가 들렸습니다.

"웬 사람들이지, 혹시 도둑떼가 아닌가?" 아우는 덜컥 겁이 나서 숨을 곳을 찾아보았습니다.

그러다가 마루에 있는 대들보 위로 재빨리 기어올라갔습니다. "으하하하 낄낄낄……."

한무리의 사람들이 왁자지껄 하며 집으로 들어왔습니다.

가만히 내려다보던 아우는 깜짝 놀라서 하마터면 떨어질 뻔했습니다.

그 무리는 사람들이 아니라 머리에 뿔이 달린 도깨비들이었습니다. 아우는 겁이 나서 부들부들 떨었습니다.

"자, 이제 슬슬 놀아 볼까?"

도깨비들은 방망이로 마룻바닥을 둥당둥당 두드리며 노래를 부르기 시작했습니다.

금 나와라, 뚝딱! 얼쑤. 은 나와라, 뚝딱! 얼쑤.

"Gold, gold, come ye forth!

Oh, silver, come ye out!"

And every time the ogres hit their clubs on something, gold and silver coins shot out. The young man watched in fascination as the ogres played their greedy game. They were having so much fun that they started to skip about and dance, all the time singing their magic song and striking things with their clubs.

The young man had forgotten his fear, but he suddenly realized that he was quite hungry.

Without a second thought, he took out one of the hazelnuts and tried to break it open with his teeth.

"Crack!" The hazelnut broke open.

The ogres stopped in their tracks. "What was that loud noise?" one of them exclaimed.

"Oh! We must have hit the cottage too many times! It must be falling down!" a second ogre cried.

"Hurry! Run! Get out before the house falls down on us!" yelled a third ogre.

And the ogres all rushed out of the house as fast as they could run.

The young man heard the ogres shout. Because he didn't know his nut-cracking had scared them, he was frightened again and very confused. He stayed right where he was on top of the beam. Looking down, though, he could see the magic clubs which the ogres had left.

도깨비들이 방망이를 두드릴 때마다 금과 은이 좌르르 쏟아져 나왔습니다. 아우는 도깨비들의 놀이에 흠뻑 빠져들어갔습니다. 흥에 겨운 도깨비들은 덩실덩실 춤까지 추었습니다.

무서움도 다 잊은 아우는 슬슬 배가 고파졌습니다. 아우는 자기도 모르게 개암 한 개를 꺼내어 깨물었습니다.

"따악!" 신나게 놀던 도깨비들은 갑자기 우뚝 멈춰 섰습니다.

"이게 무슨 소리지?"

"이크! 집이 무너지는 소리 아냐?" "어서 도망가자!"

도깨비들은 우르르 집 밖으로 뛰어나갔습니다.

아우는 겁이 나고 어리둥절하여 가만히 대들보 위에 엎드려 있었습니다.

마루 위에는 도깨비들이 버리고 간 금방망이들이 어지럽게 널려 있었습니다.

When the morning sunbeams started to glow through the door, the young man, who had slept all night curled up on the beam, finally decided to come down. Gold and silver coins covered the entire floor.

The young man laughed as he thought, "What foolish ogres! They left the cottage without taking any of their riches with them."

Then, just for fun, he picked up one of the clubs and hit it against the floor. As he did so, he repeated the words that he had heard the ogres sing.

"Gold, gold. Come ye forth!"

And, just as the club hit the floor, gold coins came pouring out. So he took the ogre's magic club home with him. The young man became very rich. His older brother, who was very greedy and lazy, was unbearably jealous of his brother's wealth. One day, the older brother lazily wandered up the mountain to gather wood, as his younger brother had done. When he got to the forest, he stretched out on the path and took a nap.

The day slowly got dark.

When the older brother finally started to wake up, a hazelnut landed with a thud right in front of him. "Hee, hee. This will taste good. I'll eat it later."

이윽고 아침 햇살이 퍼지기 시작했습니다. 밤새 대들보 위에 웅크리고 있던 아우는 그제서야 마루로 내려왔습니다. 마루 위에는 도깨비들이 버리고 간 보물들이 가득했습니다. "도깨비들은 참 어리석구나. 이 많은 보물들을 그냥 버리고 가다니……."

아우는 싱글벙글 웃으며 장난삼아 금방망이를 두드려 보았습니다.

"금 나와라, 뚝딱!" 그러자 금이 좌르르 쏟아져 나왔습니다. 아우는 도깨비방망이를 가지고 집으로 돌아왔습니다.

아우는 엄청난 부자가 되었습니다. 형은 부자가 된 아우를 보자 샘이 나서 견딜 수가 없었습니다. 놀기만 하던 형은 지게를 지고 어슬렁어슬렁 산으로 올라갔습니다. 산에 올라간 형은 낮잠을 잤습니다. 어슴푸레 날이 저물어 갔습니다. 그제서야 형은 부시시 일어났습니다.

"떽데구르르" 그 때 마침 개암 한 개가 떨어졌습니다. "히히, 맛 좋겠다. 이따가 먹어야지."

Another hazelnut fell down.
"Wow! Look at this!" he exclaimed.
"Now I have another one to eat!"

He put it in his pocket and he continued to sit around, even though the day was growing darker and darker and he hadn't gathered any wood at all.

Soon it became very dark, and the older brother stumbled his way through the forest. He reached the small, remote cottage. When he got there, he climbed up to the beam and lay down to rest some more.

After a short while, a group of ogres rushed in.

Then they all swung their clubs in the air and shouted "whoopee" and "hurrah" as they sang:

"Gold, gold. Come ye forth! Oh, silver. Come ye out!"

The ogres jumped and danced as they pounded their clubs.

The older brother watched the scene below with keen interest. Remembering his younger brother's story, he suddenly had an idea. "If I crack open a hazelnut, I will scare away the ogres! Then all their clubs will be mine!"

형은 개암을 주머니에 집어넣고 어두워지기만 기다렸습니다. 이윽고 날이 어두워지자, 형은 외딴집을 찾아가 대들보 위에 척 올라앉았습니다. 조금 뒤에 한떼의 도깨비들이 우르르 몰려들어왔습니다.
"금 나와라, 뚝딱! 얼쑤. 은 나와라, 뚝딱! 얼쑤."
도깨비들은 방망이에 장단을 맞추어 덩실덩실 춤을 추며 놀았습니다. 형은 아래에서 벌어지고 있는 광경을 아주 재미있게 구경하였습니다.
'이제 개암을 깨물면 저 도깨비방망이는 내 것이 되겠지?'

So he took a nut from his pocket and bit down on it with all his might. There was a loud cracking sound as the hazelnut split open.

The ogres suddenly stopped playing and stood still. "What was that noise?" asked one. "I bet it was that man who played a trick on us," said another. "Come on everyone. Let's catch him!" shouted a third. The ogres started rummaging every corner of the house.

The older brother tried to stay perfectly still on the beam, but he shivered and quivered in fear.

One of the ogres saw him move and shouted, "Ah-ha! There he is!"

The older brother cried and cried as he begged, "Please, please, let me go!"

"You stupid man," they shouted. "You stole one of our clubs, and you still think we'll just let you go? Let's give him a good beating." And they hit the older brother with their clubs as hard as they could.

After the ogres beat the greedy older brother over and over, they let him leave. He returned home, sore but wiser. And he never went back to that shack in the woods again.

형은 주머니에서 개암을 꺼내 힘껏 깨물었습니다.
개암이 깨지는 소리가 '따악'하고 크게 났습니다.
도깨비들은 놀이를 멈추고 우뚝 섰습니다.
"이게 무슨 소리지 ?"
"그놈이 또 왔어 !" "어서 그놈을 잡아라 !"
도깨비들은 온 집 안을 샅샅이 뒤지기 시작했습니다.
형은 대들보 위에서 꼼짝도 못하고 덜덜 떨었습니다.
"아하, 바로 저기 있었구나 !"
도깨비 하나가 형을 찾아냈습니다.
"아이고, 제발 살려 주십시오."
형은 울면서 싹싹 빌었습니다.
"네 이놈 ! 우리 방망이를 훔쳐가고도 성할 줄
알았느냐 ? 어디 혼 좀 나 봐라."
도깨비들은 형을 펑펑 두들겨팼습니다.
욕심장이 형은 실컷 매만 맞고 울면서 집으로 돌아왔습니다.
그리고 두 번 다시 숲 속의 오두막을 찾아가지 않았습니다.

On the Morning it Snowed

A poem by Pak Mogwol

On the morning it snowed
The hills in front of our village
Suddenly looked nearer than before:
The ridges covered with snow
Stood closer before me.

The footprints of peasants
At the base of the footpaths,
Between the rice paddies,
Reflected the sunlight
Like green bamboo leaves.

I went to call on my friends
Earlier on that morning.
Standing in front of the picket gate
Covered with white snow, I called
Chang-su, Tŏk-su, let's go to school!

There was no answer;
Only a hairy, puppy dog barked
As snow piled
On the persimmon tree
Branches crashed down.

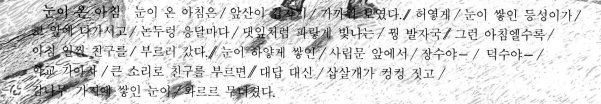

눈이 온 아침 눈이 온 아침은 / 앞산이 갑자기 / 가까와 모였다.∥ 허옇게 / 눈이 쌓인 등성이가 / 한 앞에 다가서고 / 논두렁 응달마다 / 댓잎처럼 파랗게 빛나는 / 꿩 발자국∥ 그런 아침엘수록 / 아침 일찍 친구를 / 부르러 갔다.∥ 눈이 하얗게 쌓인 / 사립문 앞에서 / 장수야— / 덕수야— / 학교 가아자 / 큰 소리로 친구를 부르면∥ 대답 대신 / 삽살개가 컹컹 짖고 / 감나무 가지에 쌓인 눈이 / 와르르 무너졌다.

56

This article is borrowed from the "Guide for Life" in the 5th grade textbook for primary schools, published by the Ministry of Education.

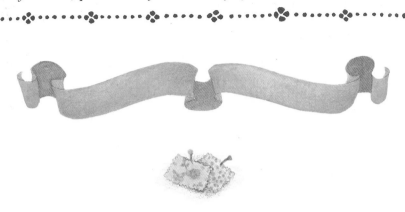

My Friendship, My Motherland

THE one who awakened my feelings for my motherland was Elijah. He was a foreigner like me.

Elijah was a boy of my age whom I met when my family immigrated to the United States and settled here. Through him I came to develop affectionate feelings toward my motherland. He not only taught me how students who immigrated to this country should live, but he also told me how he felt about the country of his birth which he left behind, and he always said that he would answer the call if it ever needed him.

Since we came to know each other, Elijah showed his interest in my own native country of Korea. He seemed as sorry for the division of Korea into north and south as if Korea was his own native land. He showed his surprise for Korea's fast economic growth, but not without some envy. As time passed and we grew up, so did our friendship grow deeper. Although we went to different universities, we got together and talked about many things whenever we could.

One day he came to me with a sad face, and said that war had broken out in his country.

"Is that true," I said. "Are you sure you want to go back there not knowing whether you will live or die?"

"This country is rich and has abundant natural resources and great potentials," he said. "As we have studied at School," he continued, "this is one of the most beautiful countries in the world. But my native country is a poor one. Maybe it is the weakest and most incapable country. But no matter how weak and poor my motherland may be, how can I turn away when it is in trouble?" After saying this, he left me and went away.

I waited every day for a word from him, looking into my mailbox every time I returned home from school. A year passed, but I did not hear from him.

Today, I looked into the empty mailbox and returned to my room. After thinking about Elijah and wishing for his safety, I realized that I too should do something good for my motherland, and decided to write a letter to young children there expressing my thoughts and feelings. I thought that this would make Elijah happy too. His love for his motherland awakened my love for my own native country. His thoughts became my thoughts.

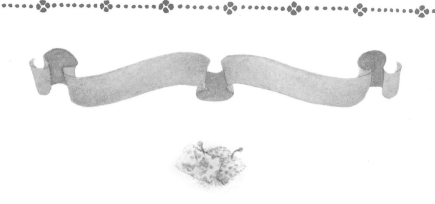

　　나에게 처음으로 조국을 일깨워 준 사람은 이 곳에서는 나와 마찬가지로 이방인인 일리어스였습니다. 일리어스는 내가 이 곳으로 이민 왔을 때 만난 나와 같은 또래의 한 소년입니다. 나는 그 소년과의 만남을 통해 조국에 대해 깊은 애착을 갖게 되었습니다.

　　그는 이민 온 학생들이 어떻게 생활해야 하는지를 모범적으로 보여주었습니다. 그러면서도 자신이 떠나온 조국에 대하여 대단한 자부심을 가지고 있었습니다. 그는 조국이 자신을 필요로 하면 언제라도 조국으로 달려가겠다는 말을 빼놓지 않았습니다.

　　일리어스는 나를 알고부터 한국에 대하여 많은 관심을 보였습니다. 남북이 단절된 한국에 대해 그는 마치 한국이 제 나라인 양 안타까워했습니다. 한국의 경제발전에 대해서는 놀라움을 금치 못하며 부러워하기도 했습니다.

　　우리의 우정은 날이 갈수록 깊어졌습니다. 그 후 우리는 각기 다른 대학에 진학했지만 시간이 나는대로 만나서 서로 많은 이야기를 나누었습니다. 그런데 하루는 그가 침울한 표정으로 나를 찾아왔습니다. 일리어스의 조국에 전쟁이 일어났다는 것입니다.

　　"그게 정말이니? 정말 죽을지 살지도 모르는 전쟁터로 가겠단 말이야?"

　　"이 나라는 많은 자원과 재산을 함께 지닌, 엄청난 가능성을 가진 나라야. 우리가 학교에서 배운대로 세계에서 가장 아름다운 나라 중의 하나일 거야. 그것에 비하면 나를 낳아 준 조국은 보잘것없는 나라지. 어쩌면 가장 못생기고 능력이 없는 어머니일지도 몰라.

　　그렇지만 아무리 못생기고 허약한 어머니일지라도 나를 낳아 주신 어머니가 고난을 겪고 있다면 그 어머니를 못 본 척할 수 있을까?" 일리어스는 나에게 그렇게 되묻고는 내 곁을 떠났습니다. 나는 그 후, 일리어스로부터 혹시 어떤 소식이라도 있나 하고 학교에서 돌아올 때마다 우편함을 꼭 뒤져 보는 버릇이 생겼습니다. 벌써 1년이 다 되어 가지만 그에게서는 아무 소식도 없었습니다.

　　나는 오늘도 우편함을 살펴보고 방으로 들어왔습니다. 내내 일리어스의 안전을 생각하다가 나도 조국을 위해 무언가를 할 수 있는 사람이 되어야겠다는 생각이 들었습니다. 이 생각 저 생각을 하다가, 조국의 어린이들에게 나의 마음을 전하기로 했습니다. 그러면 일리어스도 기뻐할 것 같습니다. 일리어스의 마음이 곧 내 마음이기 때문입니다.

National Flag

Korea's national flag is called *t'aegŭkki*. It is the symbol of Korea's sovereignty and dignity. The Korean people spilled much blood and went through many hardships to protect this flag. The symbols on this flag represent the meaning of peace, unity, creativity, and light.

대한민국의 국기는 태극기입니다.
태극기는 한국의 권위와 존엄을 표시하는 상징입니다. 그렇기 때문에 한국인은 태극기를 지키기 위하여 많은 어려움을 당하였고, 피도 많이 흘렸습니다.
태극기에는 평화·통일·창조·광명의 뜻이 담겨 있습니다.

National Flower

Korea's national flower is *mugunghwa*. Its Western name is the Rose of Sharon. Some call it *hibiscus*. The Rose of Sharon has been blooming everywhere in the Korean Peninsula from ancient times. It is a beautiful flower and its blooming season is long.

Korea's highest medal for meritorious service is called the Grand Medal of Mugunghwa, and all certificates and citations for highest awards have the design of this flower.

대한민국의 나라꽃은 무궁화입니다. 무궁화는 옛날부터 한반도 어디서나 피는 모습을 볼 수 있습니다. 꽃이 아름답고 꽃피는 기간이 길어서 한국인의 오랜 사랑을 받아온 꽃입니다.
대한민국의 최고의 훈장은 무궁화 대훈장이며, 최고의 표창도 무궁화 모양으로 되어 있습니다.

National Anthem

Korea's national anthem is called *aegukka*, which means patriotic song. It is sung loudly in unison whether it is a happy or a sad occasion. It is a prayer for Korea's well-being and development, and it is a pledge for the people's love for their country and strong determination to build an ever better nation.

애국가는 대한민국의 국가로서 나라를 사랑하는 노래입니다. 기쁠 때나 슬플 때나 다같이 소리 높여 부르는 노래입니다. 나라의 발전을 기원하는 한국인의 뜻이 담겨 있으며, 더 좋은 나라를 만들겠다는 굳은 의지와 나라 사랑하는 마음이 깃들어 있습니다.

The National Anthem

애국가

Music: *An Ik*-t'ae

Tong-hae- mul-gwa Paek-tu- sa- nı Ma-rū-go-dal - t'o Rok —
동 해 물 과 백 두 산 이 마 르 고 닳 도 록

Ha - nŭ-ni-mi Po- u-u-ha-sa U - rı-na-ra-man Se —
하 느 님 이 보 우 — 하 사 우 리 나 라 만 세

Mu - u-gung-hwa Sa - am-ch'ŏl-li Hwa-ryŏ-ga-ang San —
무 — 궁 화 삼 — 천 리 화 려 강 — 산

Tae - han-sa-ram Tae-ha-an-ŭ - ro Ki - ri- bo-jŏn-ha Se —
대 한 사 람 대 한 — 으 로 길 이 보 전 하 세

The National Anthem

1. Until the East Sea's waves are dry, and Mt. Paektu worn away,
God watch o'er our land forever! Our Korea manse!

REFRAIN:
Rose of Sharon, thousand miles of range and river land!
Guarded by her people, ever may Korea stand!

2. Like that South Mountain armored pine, standing on duty still,
wind or frost, unchanging ever, be our resolute will.

3. In autumn's arching evening sky, crystal, and cloudless blue,
Be the radiant moon our spirit, steadfast, single, and true.

4. With such a will, and such a spirit, loyalty, heart and hand,
Let us love, come grief, come gladness, this, our beloved land!

Hero of the War Between Korea and Japan

From his childhood, Yi Sun-shin was upright in character, and he never fell into temptation for power. He was a loyal subject who devoted his life to his country. He was the war hero who invented the world's first iron-clad battle ships, humiliated Japanese troops and won many famous naval victories, and served his country well.

In 1592, when Yi Sun-shin was commander of coastal security of Chŏlla Province, the Japanese invaded Korea and started war. The war started in the year named Imjin, so it was called the Imjin Japanese War. With the ambition to conquer China, some 150,000 Japanese warriors invaded Korea first. As a result, Korean farmlands were ruined, thousands of people were killed, and many houses were destroyed by Japanese soldiers. The war lasted seven years.

Admiral Yi Sun-shin had trained his troops, repaired ships, and built the unique iron-clad warships called "turtle boats." They could easily go among the enemy ships and attack them.

A great naval battle took place when the Japanese navy moved north from the South Sea to the Yellow Sea along the southern coast to supply weapons, food and other war materials to their land troops which had penetrated deeply into the interior of Korea. With his strong patriotism, brave spirit, and deep sense of responsibility to protect his country, Admiral Yi himself directed his troops in the important sea battle. Using his knowledge about the direction of wind and sea currents in the South Sea off the southern coast of the Korean Peninsula, he destroyed many Japanese warships, cut off Japanese supply lines with his turtle boats, and won a major naval victory. His victory turned the tide of the war. While fighting the Japanese toward the end of the seven-year war, Admiral Yi was wounded by enemy bullets, and died at the age of 53.

Many compare Admiral Yi Sun-shin to the English naval hero, Admiral Nelson, because both of them fought bravely for their country and died in battle shortly before the victory drum sound was heard. However, many have a greater respect and admiration for Admiral Yi Sun-shin's spirit of dedication and patriotic action. This is because, while Admiral Nelson died as commander-in-chief of the British expeditionary force, Yi Sun-shin died as a common soldier after losing his rank and position because of a wicked plot of political rivals against him.

1592년 이순신이 전라도 해안경비와 책임을 맡고 있을 때 임진왜란이 일어났습니다.

일본군은 이웃 나라에 욕심을 내어 15만의 군사로 한국을 침략하였습니다. 이리하여 한국의 국토는 일본군에 의해 짓밟히고 말았습니다.

전쟁이 일어나기 전 이순신은 이미 일본의 침입을 예견하여 군사를 훈련시키고 병선을 수리하는데 힘썼습니다.

또 적선을 향하여 거침없이 나아갈 수 있는 거북선과 같은 전함을 만들었습니다.

일본 해군은 한국의 남해를 거쳐 황해로 올라가 그들의 육군에게 전쟁물자를 대주려고 하였습니다. 그렇기 때문에 바다에서의 싸움은 전쟁의 승패를 좌우할 만큼 중요했습니다.

이순신은 나라를 지켜야한다는 애국심과 용감한 정신으로 전투에 앞장서 지휘함으로써 매번 승리를 거두었습니다.

또한 반도와 만이 복잡한 남해안의 지형과 바닷물의 흐름을 잘 이용하여 뛰어난 전술을 세웠습니다. 그리고는 일본군이 한국으로 들어올 수 있는 통로를 완전히 끊어 버렸습니다.

이순신은 7년에 걸친 한 · 일전쟁이 끝날 무렵 일본군을 무찌르던 중, 적군의 총탄에 맞아 53세를 끝으로 전사했습니다.

이순신을 흔히 영국의 넬슨 제독과 비교하는 사람들이 많이 있습니다.

위기에 빠진 조국을 구하고 승리의 북소리가 울리기 직전에 전사한 넬슨의 생애는, 한국의 이순신과 비슷한 점이 많기 때문입니다.

그러나 해군 총사령관이라는 최고의 지위를 갖고 영국에 승리를 안겨준 넬슨보다, 갖은 모함으로 모든 지위를 빼앗기고도 불평하지 않고, 오직 나라를 위한 일에 목숨을 바치고자 했던 이순신의 위대한 정신과 행동은 많은 사람들에게 감동을 안겨줍니다.

The Half-moon

A children's song by Yun Kŭk-yŏng

The Milky Way and a small, white boat
With a cinnamon tree and a rabbit
In the blue sky.
Without a sail or an oar
It sails through the sky swiftly
Toward the western land.

반 달 푸른 하늘 은하수 하얀 쪽배에 / 계수나무 한 나무 토끼 한 마리 /
돛대도 아니 달고 삿대도 없이 / 가기도 잘도 간다 서쪽 나라로

Oh! The Cries of That Day

March the first is Korea's memorial day for the March First Movement of 1919 which was the first nationwide independence movement.

In 1910, Korea sadly lost its independence to Japan. Because the Japanese ruled Korea with military might and oppressed its poeple, Koreans could not live peacefully. Many Koreans were put in prison while many of them were forced to leave their native land for foreign countries.

As masters in Korea, the Japanese took away the freedom of Koreans to speak the Korean language, study their history, or to gather together and talk about their future. They were not allowed to sing their patriotic songs or show their national flag. Day by day, the police rule of the Japanese increased. In this situation, the desire of the Koreans to regain their freedom and liberty from the brutal Japanese grew steadily while the leaders in Korea met secretly and talked about the ways to regain the independence of Korea. Secretly, they produced the Korean flag, wrote the Declaration of Independence, and distributed them throughout Korea.

Finally, the day arrived. The torch light of patriotism was lit, signaling the beginning of a great movement that was about to start.

1910년, 한국은 불행하게도 일본에게 나라의 주권을 강제로 빼앗기고 말았습니다. 일본은 무력으로써 지배하고 탄압하였기 때문에 한국의 국민들은 마음놓고 살 수가 없었습니다. 한국의 많은 사람들이 감옥에 갇히거나 멀리 외국으로 떠나야했습니다. 일본은 한국 땅에서 주인 행세를 하며, 한국의 말과 글은 물론 함께 모여 의논할 자유까지 박탈했습니다.

날이 갈수록 일본 경찰과 헌병들의 탄압은 심해졌습니다. 이러한 폭력과 강권으로부터, 짓밟힌 자유를 되찾겠다는 생각이 한국 국민들 사이에서 용솟음치기 시작했습니다.

독립운동가들은 일본의 눈을 피해 나라를 되찾으려는 일을 의논하고 태극기를 만들었으며, 독립선언서를 지어서 전국에 돌렸습니다.

드디어 그 날이 다가왔습니다.

나라 사랑의 큰 뜻이 담긴 횃불이 밤하늘에 솟아오른 것입니다. 그 횃불은 내일 있을 일을 다짐하는, 미리 약속된 신호였습니다.

As the dawn of March 1, 1919 arrived, the people were ready for action. They hid their forbidden national flag inside their clothes and quietly waited for the time for action.

At noon, the people who gathered in the Pagoda Park in downtown Seoul heard the voice of a young teacher who read the Declaration of Independence, and said:

"My fellow countrymen, we the people who have more than 4,000 years of glorious history have been trampled on by the Japanese. The Japanese have stolen our country, and they have taken away our independence.

"We must recover our country and our independence. The cries for independence are rising in every nook and corner of our land. We must recover

1919년 3월 1일, 날이 밝았습니다. 사람들은 옷 속에 태극기를 감추고 떨리는 마음으로 말없이 때를 기다리고 있었습니다.

정오가 되었습니다. 그러자,

"여러분, 4천 년의 빛나는 역사를 가진 우리 겨레가 왜놈들에게 짓밟히고 있습니다. 우리는 나라를 빼앗겼습니다. 이제 나라를 되찾아야합니다. 지금 전국 방방곡곡에서 독립을 외치고 있습니다.

여러분, 나라를 되찾아야합니다. 만세를 부릅시다. 대한독립 만세를 !"

our independence. Let us shout for our independence. Let us shout for the everlasting independence of Korea!"

At that moment the cries of "Long Live Korea! Long Live Korean Independence" were heard all over the country as the people took out their national flag and marched in the streets, waving it high. "Long Live Korea! Long Live Korean Independence!" they shouted, shaking heaven and earth.

Waves of national flags filled the streets as the people marched. Young and old, men and women everywhere joined the march. All the people who had Korean blood marched as they shouted "Long Live Korea! Long Live Korean Independence!"

열여섯 살 소녀의 이같은 외침에 사람들은 눈이 빛나기 시작했습니다.
모두가 옷 속에서, 감추었던 태극기를 꺼내 들었습니다.
"만세! 만세!"
"대한독립 만세!"
만세소리가 하늘과 땅을 흔들었습니다. 태극기의 물결이 거리를 가득 메웠습니다.
태극기를 휘두르고 대한독립 만세를 외치는 시가행진은 계속되었습니다. 도시에서, 각 고을마다, 거리마다
할아버지 할머니 어른 아이 할 것 없이 한국 사람의 피를 받은 사람이면 모두 뛰어나와 만세를 불렀습니다.

The Japanese military and police tried to block the people's demonstrations with their bayonets. Some mounted police charged into the crowds. The people kept on marching as they spilled their blood. Their cries became louder. Hundreds of people were killed by the Japanese soldiers and police. Thousands of them were arrested and tortured. But they did not give up. A young girl student stood bravely and shouted at the Japanese police: "What is wrong with our crying for our national independence? You have no right to kill us, arrest us, or torture us. I am a daughter of Korea!"

The leaders of the independence movement were imprisoned and tortured, but the Japanese could not crush the patriotism and determination of the Korean people to recover their national independence.

The cries of Koreans shook the world as they demonstrated their spirit of nationalism that was alive in their body and soul. The world learned that Koreans were a people who would sacrifice their lives for freedom and liberty, and for the recovery of their country's independence.

Much time has passed since that day, but today Koreans still demonstrate the same spirit. They will keep the same spirit forever.

일본 경찰과 헌병들이 총칼과 말굽으로 전진하는 군중들을 막으려 했습니다.

그러나 피를 흘리며 쓰러져가면서도 태극기의 행렬은 멈추지 않았고 겨레의 함성은 계속해서 울려 퍼졌습니다. 많은 사람들이 죽어갔으며 일본 헌병들에게 끌려갔습니다.

끌려간 사람들은 이루 말할 수 없는 고문을 당하였습니다.

"내 나라를 사랑하여 독립 만세를 부른 것이 무슨 잘못이오! 당신들은 나를 심문할 자격이 없소. 나는 어엿한 대한의 딸이란 말이오."

나이 어린 소녀는 한치도 물러섬이 없이 당당하게 말하였습니다.

한국의 독립운동가들은 감옥 속에서 모진 고문을 당했지만 독립을 바라는 뜻은 그 누구도 꺾을 수가 없었습니다.

일본의 심한 감시와 탄압을 받으면서도 온 국민이 만세를 불러 세상을 뒤흔들게 된 것은 한국인의 핏줄기와 가슴 속에 흐르는 민족정신이 있었기 때문입니다.

한국인은 무엇보다도 자주성을 중요하게 여기며 이를 지키기 위해서는 목숨을 걸고 항쟁하는 민족임을 세계

여러 나라에서 알게 되었습니다. 지금도 한국 사람들은 그 정신 속에서 살고 있으며, 영원히 살아갈 것입니다.

These quotations were taken from his Glimpses of World History; Being Further Letters to his Daughter, Written in Prison, and Containing a Rambling Account of History for Young People. *New York: The John Day Company, 1942, pp. 117, 118, 465.*

Jawaharlal Nehru's Letters to his Daughter, Indira

While he was struggling for India's independence, Jawaharlal Nehru, who later became the first prime minister of the independent India, wrote many letters from prison cells to his daughter, Indira, who also served India as prime minister after the death of her father. In his letters, Nehru mentioned Korea on many times.

In one of his letters dated May 8, 1932, he wrote that "Korea produced beautiful works of art, especially of sculpture.... Great progress was made in shipbuilding." However, he said that "Korea, poor, little country, is almost forgotten today. Japan has swallowed her up and made her part of her empire. But Korea dreams still of freedom and struggles for independence."

Regarding Korea's struggle for independence after Japan annexed her in 1910, Nehru said the following in his letter dated December 30, 1932:

"The Japanese brought some modern reforms with them, but they ruthlessly crushed the spirit of the Korean people. For many years the struggle for independence continued and there were many outbreaks, the most important one being in 1919.

"The people of Korea, especially young men and women, struggled gallantly against tremendous odds... they sacrificed themselves for their ideology. The suppression of the Koreans by the Japanese is a very sad and dark chapter in history. You will be interested to know that young Korean girls, many of them fresh from college, played a prominent part in the struggle."

"위대한 문화유산을 가진 나라, 코리아. 일본은 어느 정도 한국에 근대적 개혁을 가져왔으나 한국민중의 정신을 유린하고 문화를 말살하려 했다. 이에 분개한 한국 사람들은 여러 차례 독립항쟁을 하였다. 그 중에서 가장 큰 항쟁이 1919년에 일어났다. 코리아의 민중, 특히 젊은이들은 무장한 적에 맨몸으로 용감히 투쟁하였다. 그들이 자유를 되찾기 위해 독립을 선언하고 일본에 항거했을 때 수없이 많은 사람이 구속되어 고문을 당하고 죽어갔다. 그들은 그들의 이상을 위해 희생하고 순국했던 것이다. 한국에서 흔히 학생들이 또는 대학을 갓 나온 젊은 여성들이 투쟁의 중요한 역활을 맡는다는 사실을 알게 되면 너도 틀림없이 감동을 받을 것이다."

To "The Kings in My Heart"

The following is an excerpt from a message which the Romanian writer who later sought refuge in France, Constant-Virgil Gheorghiu, sent to the South Korean people in 1972. Gheorghiu's most important work Vingt-cinquième heure *is famed throughout the world. In 1974 he visited Korea and gave a lecture to the Korean people. This message, originally written in French, was translated into Korean. This excerpt is from the Korean version of his message.*

You have lived through a long history of trials and tribulations, but you are not pitiable losers. Each one of you is the king. Do not forget this. Those of the powerful countries who commit aggression and impose their domination over others may not know that you are the kings.

Those who live in large countries, in the glory of victory, in wealth and boredom may not know the beauty of humanitarian love of those who hold hands and offer their sympathies to each other. They may not know the happiness that is created from hardships.

Have courage. Even the history of hardships could not take away your beautiful poetry, songs, and prayers. You possess the soul that the world has lost.

You, who possess the soul of the king! What you have created are not refrigerators, television sets, or automobiles. What you have created are the everlasting smiles and peace for mankind which could overcome earthly things and shed bright light. What I have said about the east from which the light may come may very well mean the small country of Korea where you live. There should be no surprise if one said that the tomorrow's light will rise from your country of Korea. It is so because you are the people who have overcome countless hardships and come out victorious from each hardship. You are the people who raised your heads high with bravery, wisdom, and inner strength in the midst of trials and tribulations.

여러분은 오랜 수난의 역사 속에서 살아왔습니다.

그러나 여러분은 비참한 패자가 아니라 오히려 한 사람 한 사람 모두가 왕자입니다.

잊지 마십시오.

남을 침략하고 지배하는 강대국의 사람들은 여러분이 여전히 왕자라는 것을 모를 것입니다.

땅이 넓은 나라의 사람들, 승리의 영광 속에 사는 사람들, 풍요 속에서 하품을 하고 사는 사람들은 서로 만나서 위로하고 손을 마주 잡는 인정의 아름다움을 모를 것입니다. 고난에서 생겨나는 창조의 기쁨을 모를 것입니다.

여러분, 용기를 가지십시오.

고난의 역사도 결코 당신들의 아름다운 시와 노래와 기도를 빼앗아 가지는 못하였습니다.

당신들은 세계가 잃어버린 영혼을 가지고 있습니다.

왕자의 영혼을 지니고 사는 여러분!

당신들이 창조한 것은, 냉장고와 TV와 자동차가 아니라 지상의 것을 극복하고 거기에 밝은 빛을 던지는 영원한 미소와 인류의 평화입니다.

내가 빛이 온다고 말한 그 동방은 여러분들의 작은 나라 한국에 잘 적용되는 말입니다.

내일의 빛이 한국에서 비쳐온다 해도 놀랄 것은 조금도 없습니다. 왜냐하면 여러분은 수많은 고난을 겪어온 민족이며 그 고통을 번번히 이겨낸 민족이기 때문입니다.

당신들은 고난을 스스로의 용기와 슬기와 힘으로 이겨낸 사람들이기 때문입니다.

Seoul Olympiad

On September 30, 1981, at Baden Baden, Germany, it was decided to have the 1988 Summer Olympic Games in Seoul, Korea.
This news surprised Koreans and made them very proud.
It would be the second time for the Summer Olympic Games to be held in an Asian nation. The first time was in Tokyo, Japan, in 1964.

1981년 9월 30일, 서독의 바덴바덴, "Seoul，Korea！"
1988년 올림픽 대회의 개최지로 한국의 서울이 결정되었을 때 한국 국민들은 놀라움과 자부심을 느꼈습니다. 서울 올림픽은 1964년 일본의 동경 올림픽에 이어 아시아에서는 두번째로 열리게 된 것입니다.

The Korean people were able to have a common goal by having such an important event as the Summer Olympiad in Seoul. It nurtured patriotism and cooperative spirit, and it was an event that united Koreans both at home and abroad. As a result, they won 12 gold, 10 silver and 11 bronze medals to rank fourth in a field of 160 nations in the 1988 Seoul Olympics.

The Seoul Olympiad was a peaceful and harmonious festival of the peoples of the world. Not only that, during the Seoul Olympic Games, an international festival was held where many cultures of the world met and promoted friendly exchanges.

서울 올림픽과 같은 큰 행사를 통해서 한국 국민들은 공동의 목표를 갖게 되었습니다. 그것은 한국 국민들에게 애국심과 협동심을 북돋아 주었으며, 나라 안의 국민들은 물론 나라 밖의 국민들까지도 하나로 뭉치게 하는 겨레의 대행사였습니다. 서울 올림픽은 세계 160여개국이 함께 참가한 세계 평화와 화합의 축제였습니다. 이 대회에서 한국은 세계 제 4위의 기록을 얻었습니다. 뿐만 아니라, 전 세계의 다양한 문화가 서로 만나고, 교류되는 문화 올림픽도 함께 열렸습니다.

The Seoul Olympiad brought out in the Korean people a new awareness of their own culture. At the same time, it gave them an opportunity to let the world know about Korean culture and develop an interest in it. Consequently, the Western people who used to call Korea "The Land of the Morning Calm" now call it the "country with a wonderful culture," or the "country of progress and growth."

Most of all, in the Seoul Olympiad the Free World countries and the Socialist countries developed friendly and harmonious relations. Many monuments were erected in the Olymic Park in Seoul in the name of peace. Among them was the "Gate of Peace" which will be an everlasting symbol of hope for the peaceful coexistence of the peoples of the world without the fear of threat of war.

서울 올림픽은 한국 국민들로 하여금 한국 문화예술에 대해 다시 한번 생각하게 해주었습니다. 그리고 세계 여러 나라로 하여금 한국에 대한 관심을 갖도록 함과 동시에 이를 전 세계에 전파하는 중요한 계기가 되었습니다. 한국을 '조용한 아침의 나라'라고 불렀던 외국 사람들이 이제는 '발전과 성장의 나라', '무한한 가능성이 있는 나라'라고 말하고 있습니다.

서울 올림픽은 무엇보다도 자유진영과 공산진영의 여러 나라들이 한자리에 모여서 화해하고 우의를 다지는 자리였습니다. 이 한마당 잔치에 즈음하여 올림픽 공원에는 많은 기념물들이 평화의 이름으로 세워졌습니다. 그 중에서도 '평화의 문'은 전쟁과 폭력의 위협없이 온 인류가 평화롭게 살기를 갈망하는 상징으로 자손만대에 물려줄 기념물입니다.

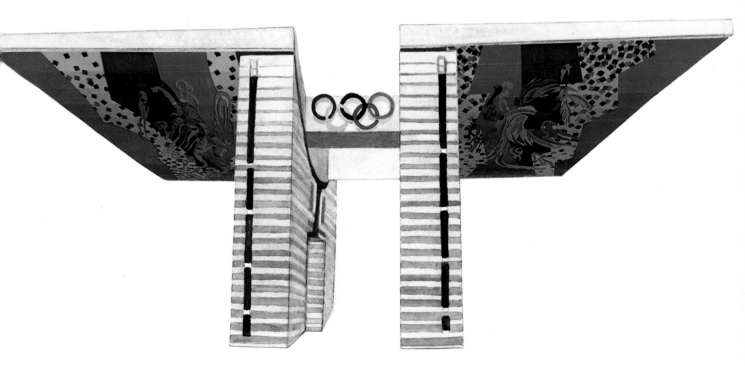

Hand in Hand

Music: Giorgio Moroder
Korean lyrics: Kim Mun-whan
English lyrics: Tom Whitlock

See the fi-re — in the sky ——————— We
This is our time — to rise a - bove We

1.

feel the beat-ing of our hearts to ge-ther———
know the chance is here to live for

2.

e ——— ver For - all time ——————— Hand in

76

hand we stand ——— all a – cross the land We can make this world
hand we can start to un – der-stand break-ing down the walls

1.
— a bet — ter place in which to li — ve ——— Hand in
that come be – tween us for all

2.
time ——————— A - ri - rang ———

손에 손잡고

하늘 높이 솟는 불 우리들 가슴 고동치게 하네
이제 모두 다 일어나 영원히 함께 살아가야 할 길
나서자 손에 손잡고 벽을 넘어서
우리 사는 세상 더욱 살기 좋도록 ……
손에 손잡고 벽을 넘어서
서로 서로 사랑하는 한마음 되자 손잡고

'93 Taejŏn Expo

TAEJŎN is a city approximately 170 kilometers south of Seoul, the capital of Korea. The city is a transportation hub, so it is always abuzz with activity, with people and goods on the move. However, in the late summer and autumn of 1993, it saw the coming and going of more people than ever because of the 1993 International Exposition it hosted.

About 14 million people visited the '93 Taejŏn Expo during its 93-day run. A record 108 countries and 33 organizations participated in this olympics of science, technology, art and culture whose theme was "The Challenge of a New Road to Development."

Perhaps it is only fitting that a new road to development was pursued in the Taejŏn Expo because Taejŏn, a transportation hub, has long been a place where people have come to take another road, to take another direction. The Expo showed that the new road to development requires a harmonizing of modern science and traditional technology and cooperation and sharing between the advanced countries and the developing countries. It also showed that the new road must lead to a solution for the problems of pollution and depletion of natural resources that are caused by industrialization.

The Taejŏn Expo will be long remembered for providing a vision for a road to lead to greater prosperity for all mankind in the 21st century.

서울에서 남쪽으로 약 170km 떨어진 대전시는 교통의 중심지로서 늘 오가는 사람들이 많은 곳입니다. 특히 1993년의 여름과 가을은 경제·과학·문화의 올림픽이라고도 불리는 엑스포가 개최되어 1천 4백만명의 관람객이 다녀갔습니다.

108개 나라와 33개의 국제기구가 참가한 가운데 93일간 펼쳐진 '93 대전엑스포는 선진국과 개발도상국이 가지고 있는 현대과학과 전통 기술의 조화를 모색하며 산업화 과정에서 생기는 공해와 자원문제를 해결할 수 있는 방향을 전시 함으로써 새로운 도약에의 길을 제시했습니다.

Seoul, Korea's Capital for 600 Years

1994 is a significant year for Seoul. It is the six-hundredth anniversary of its establishment as the capital of Korea. The city has been the nation's capital since the late fourteenth century when Yi Sŏng-gye, King T'aejo, the first king of the newly established Chosŏn Dynasty (1392-1910), chose it as the most propitious site on the Korean Peninsula to build his new capital, which he called Hanyang.

Of course the city has undergone much change and growth since 1394. The population now exceeds ten million, or about one hundred times its population in the time of King T'aejo, and the city has expanded far beyond the city wall he constructed. However, just as it was then, it is still the center of Korea's government, economy, culture and society. Moreover, it is now known worldwide as one of the most exciting cities in Asia.

1994년은 서울이 한국의 수도로 정해진 지 600년이 되는 뜻깊은 해입니다. 1394년 이성계가 새 왕조인 조선(1392-1910)을 세우면서 한반도에서 가장 상서로운 곳으로 현재의 서울을 한양이라 칭하며 왕조의 수도로 삼았던 것입니다. 그 후 서울은 한국의 정치, 경제, 사회, 문화의 중심지로 성장과 발전을 계속하여 인구 천만이 넘는 세계적인 도시가 되었습니다.

Koreans to Remember

An Chung-gŭn (안중근 , 1897-1910), patriot.

An Ik-t'ae (안익태 , 1906-1965), musician, composer of Korean national anthem.

Chŏng Chu-yŏng (정주영 , 1915-), industrialist, founder of the Hyundai Group.

Chŏng Kyŏng-hwa (정경화 , 1948-), violinist.

Chŏng Myŏng-hun (정명훈 , 1953-), musician, conductor.

Chu Shi-gyŏng (주시경 , 1876-1914), nationalist, scholar of Korean language.

Ch'a Pŏm-gŭn (차범근 , 1953-), soccer champion.

Ch'oe Nam-sŏn (최남선 , 1890-1957), scholar, poet, author of the Declaration of Independence (1919).

Han Kyŏng-jik (한경직 , 1902-), Protestant minister.

Kim Chŏng-hŭi (김정희 , 1786-1850), calligrapher, epigraphist.

Kim Chung-ŏp (김중업 , 1922-1989), modern architect.

Kim Ch'ang-yŏl (김창열 , 1929-), modern painter.

Kim Hong-do (김홍도 , 1760-1824), genre painter.

Kim Hwal-lan (Helen Kim, 김활란 , 1899-1970), educator.

Kim Ki-ch'ang (김기창 , 1914-), traditional painter.

Kim Paek-pong (김백봉 , 1927-), ballerina, professor of Korean traditional dance.

Kim Sowol (Kim Chŏng-shik, 김소월 , 1902-1935), poet.

Kim Su-gŭn (김수근 , 1931-1986), modern architect.

Kim Su-hwan (김수환 , 1922-), Cardinal of the Roman Catholic Church.

Saint Kim Tae-gŏn Andrew (김대건 , 1822-1846), Catholic priest, martyr.

Kim U-jung (김우중 , 1936-), industrialist, founder of the Daewoo Group.

Kim Young-sam (김 영 삼**, 1927-),**
  politician, 7th President of Korea.

Kim Yu-shin (김 유 신 , 595-673), Shilla
  general, unifier of the Three Kingdoms.

Ko Sang-don (고 상 돈 , 1948-1979),
  conqueror of Mount Everest.

Lee Chung-sŏp (이 중 섭 , 1916-1956),
  modern painter.

Lee Kwang-su (이 광 수 , 1892- ?), novelist,
  writer of the first modern novel, *Mujŏng*.

Lee Mun-yŏl (이 문 열 , 1948-), novelist,
  powerful, multifaceted best-selling author.

Lee Pyŏng-ch'ŏl (이 병 철 , 1910-1987),
  industrialist, founder of the Samsung Group.

Lee Sŭng-man (Syngman Rhee, 이 승 만 ,
  1875-1965), patriot, first president of
  the Republic of Korea.

Na Un-gyu (나 운 규 , 1902-1937), movie
  actor, maker of the film *Arirang*.

Paek Nam-jun (백 남 준 , 1932-) video artist.

Pang Chŏng-hwan (방 정 환 , 1899-1931),
  writer of children's literature.

Park Chung-hee (박 정 희 , 1917-1979),
  general, president of the Republic of
  Korea, (1963-1979).

Sejong (세종대왕 , 1397-1450), Yi Dynasty
  king, creator of the *han'gŭl*
  alphabet.

Sŏ Chae-p'il (Philip Jaisohn, 서 재 필 , 1866-
  1951), nationalist, founder of the
  Independent Press, adviser to the
  Independence Club.

Son Ki-jŏng (손 기 정 , 1912-), athlete,
  winner of the gold medal in the
  marathon at the 1936 Berlin
  Olympics.

U Chang-ch'un (우 장 춘 , 1898-1959),
  agricultural scientist.

Ŭlchi Mundŏk (을지문덕 , late 6th and early
  7th century), Koguryŏ general.

Wonhyo (원 효 , 617-686), Shilla Buddhist
  scholar-monk.

Yi Sun-shin (이 순 신 , 1545-1598), admiral,
  hero of the Korean-Japanese war.

Protected Natural Monuments in Korea

The Korean government has designated certain endangered species of birds, insects, and plants and nature's creations as "protected natural monuments." Some of them are:

HWANGSAE (Crane)

IN Korean, the white stork (crane) is called *hwangsae*. It has long legs, and a long neck, and a black-colored bill. It is a migratory bird. Wading around in shallow waters it catches fish and frogs. It does not sing, but occasionally it makes a high-pitched squawk. This beautiful bird is a symbol of long life in Korea, China and Japan.

발에 물갈퀴가 조금 있고, 다리가 길어 물 위를 걸으며 물고기를 잡아 먹습니다. 다른 새들처럼 울지를 못하며 쉴 때는 한 쪽 다리로 서서 쉽니다.

MISŎN NAMU (Abelia)

WHAT the Koreans call *misŏn namu* is a rare native bush of Korea. It usually grows to 3 feet in height on the shady side of hills. Its white flower (sometimes light pink) blooms in March before leaves sprout, and it bears small berries.

세계에서 오직 하나밖에 없는 한국의 고유식물입니다. 키는 1m 미만이고, 꽃은 흰빛으로 이른 봄에 잎이 나기 전에 먼저 핍니다.

THE CHINDO DOG

THIS uniquely Korean dog is a native of the island named Chindo, off the southwest coast of Korea. A medium-sized dog, its average height is between 1 foot 11 inches and 2 feet 7 inches, and it is light yellow or near-white in color. It has pointed, upright ears, and its short tail usually curves upward, the tip touching the left side of its back. It is intelligent, obedient, and brave. Its hearing and sense of smell are extremely keen. It is popular as a house pet, as well as a police or hunting dog.

한국의 특산종입니다.
귀는 세우고 꼬리를 말고 다닙니다. 민첩하고, 슬기롭고, 용맹하며, 청각과 후각이 특히 발달되어 주로 사냥개, 경찰개로도 삼습니다.

TTAOGI (Crested Ibis)

THE Korean name for the crested ibis is *ttaogi*. It has black feathers, a long neck, and a downward-curved bill. It has long feathers at the back of its head. Living in rice paddies or ponds on hillsides, it makes "tta-oak, tta-oak" sound, so the Koreans call it *ttaogi*. It is a very shy, individualistic bird, and it avoids any contact with humans.

연못가나 깊은 삼림의 나무 위에 홀로 또는 2~10마리씩 떼지어 살며, '따옥 따옥' 하고 웁니다. 4~5월에, 나무 위에 접시 모양의 집을 짓고 두세 개의 알을 낳습니다.

K'ŬNAKSAE (Woodpecker)

KOREANS call a certain kind of woodpeckers *k'ŭnaksae*. The *k'ŭnak* bird has a shiny black back, red head and cheeks, and white chest. Usually a male and female live together in thickly wooded areas. When they hammer into wood in search of insects, the hammering sound can be heard a half mile away.

암수 한 쌍씩 무성한 밀림에서 삽니다.
뾰족한 부리를 가지고 나무를 찍어 벌레를 잡아먹습니다.
이 때 나는 소리는 매우 요란해서 1km 밖에까지 들린다고 합니다.

KONI (White Swan)

KOREANS call Eastern Bewick's swan *koni*. This large, beautiful bird is a migratory bird, spending some time on the lakes in Korea before flying further south. Living in a group, the *koni* eats water weeds, shellfish, and fish.

철새의 한 종류로 겨울새입니다. 온몸은 새하얗고 맵시가 매우 좋습니다.
호수에 떼지어 살며, 물풀, 조개, 물고기를 잡아먹습니다.

Hymn of Seoul

서울의 찬가

Music: Kil Ok-yun

Chong-i-ul-li-ne
종 이 울리 네

Kko-ch'i-p'i-ne
꽃 이 피 네

Sae-dŭ-re-no-rae
새 들의 노 래

Un-nŭn-gŭ-ŏl-kul
웃 는 그 얼 굴

Kŭ-ri-wo-ra
그 리 워 – 라

Nae-sa-rang - a
내 사 랑 – 아

Hymn of Seoul

Bells toll, flowers bloom, and songs of birds abound;
I yearn for that smiling face.
Oh, my beloved, do not leave my side.
This is where my heart is,
This is where we met and pledged our love.
I shall live in beautiful Seoul,
I shall live in Seoul.

Nae - gyŏ-tjŭl-ttŏ-na-ji-ma - O   Ch'ŏ-ŭm Man-na-sŏ-sa-rang-ŭl-mae
내　겉을떠나지마 오　　　처음 만나서사랑을맺

Jŭn　　　Chŏng-da-un-gŏ-ri-ma-ŭ-me-gŏ Ri　　　A-rŭm
은　　　정다 운 거리마음의거 리　　　아름

ta - un-sŏ-u-re-sŏ-　　　Sŏ-u-re-sŏ-sal-lyŏm-ni Ta
다　운서울에서　　　서울 에 서살렵니다.

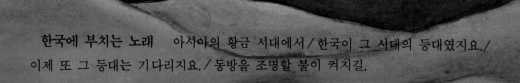

Sir Rabindranath Tagore (1861-1941) of Calcutta, India was the first Asian to win the Nobel Prize in Literature in 1913. This eminent Indian philosopher and poet wrote the following poem about Korea.

Korea

A poem by Tagore

In the golden age of Asia
Korea was one of its lamp bearers.
And that lamp is waiting
To be lighted once again
For the illumination of the East.

한국에 부치는 노래   아시아의 황금 시대에서 / 한국이 그 시대의 등대였지요. /

이제 또 그 등대는 기다리지요. / 동방을 조명할 불이 켜지길.